ELIJAH THE PROPHET

"A MAN SUBJECT TO LIKE PASSIONS AS WE ARE."
(*James* 5-17)

BY
W.W. FEREDAY

FORMERLY PUBLISHED AS ELIJAH THE TISHBITE

Author of "Our Lord's Miracles and Parables,"
Solomon and his Temple",
"Samuel : God's Emergency Man,"
"Jonah and Balaam?" etc, etc.

GW00686292

JOHN RITCHIE LTD.
PUBLISHERS OF CHRISTIAN LITERATURE
KILMARNOCK

ISBN 0-946351-15-5

Printed by Bell and Bain Ltd., Glasgow

Contents

Preface to 2nd Edition

W.W. Fereday was born in England in 1863, was saved at 16 and almost immediately started to preach. He spent the whole of his life in the study and exposition of the Scripture of Truth and was much respected and loved by the people of God. He travelled extensively and spent a considerable time in Scotland and the continent of Europe. He was a faithful expositor of the Word of God. He knew no fear and never compromised for one moment, but one could not help but love him.

He lived for many years in Rothesay, Scotland, and the last five years of his life at Machermore Eventide Home, Scotland, from where he went to be with the Lord at the age of 96. He was the last of a very worthy kind – John Nelson Darby, William Kelly, William Woldridge Fereday. Brother Fereday always had two life-size portraits of these two revered men of God in his large study, he knew them both personally and they were guides to him in his early formative years.

Many lovers of the Scriptures have spent long hours immersing themselves in the writings of J.N. Darby and have found them at first reading almost beyond understanding. However, after a further reading, the truth conveyed gradually shone through and one could grasp the writer's meaning and then would gladly acknowledge that what he wrote was undoubtedly right. On the other hand William Kelly was lengthy and laborious; he wandered into many unnecessary by-paths. An enormous number of pages had to be read in order to obtain a small portion of truth but, we hasten to add, a very sweet portion.

However W.W. Fereday was different. Precise, accurate, lucid, brief; he was as cryptic in his written ministry as in his public addresses. One of his favourite expressions was "I do not give lectures, I state facts". He never wasted a word, wrote in the briefest possible way, taught the same truths as J.N.D. and W.K. but in a language that was simple, interesting, and often thrilling; In fact just in the form that young Christians will appreciate today.

John Ritchie Limited have done a great service to the Lord's people in republishing these books in paperback. We are sure God will use them in blessing to this present generation.

A.M.S. Gooding

Foreword

HAVING published many years ago a book on "Elisha the Prophet" the question has sometimes been asked, "Why have you passed by Elijah?" No special reason can be given; but here, at long last, is a book on Elisha's distinguished predecessor. May its message be helpful to us all.

★　★　★

We are in danger of regarding the worthies of old time – especially those whose records are given us in Holy Scripture – in a false light. To the common-place people of the Twentieth Century those characters seem to have walked upon heights inaccessible to us. We look with awe at Abraham, Moses, Elijah, and Paul (to name only a few), and perhaps we feel that we can never hope to walk as they walked, and serve as they served. The ancient worthies thus become almost unreal to us.

Now the Holy Spirit has expressly guarded against this in the case of Elijah. In James 5:17 we are told that "he was a man subject to like passions as we are." This means that this remarkable man of God, whose name will never perish, was not essentially different from any present-day Christian. He was bold, certainly; but he could also be moody, nervous, and self-centred. Unlike human biographers, the Holy Spirit tells us the whole truth about the characters of whom He writes.

We must never forget that Old Testament believers were not favoured as we are. They knew God as the Almighty, and as Jehovah, but not as Father; for the Only-Begotten Son, who is in the bosom of the Father, had not yet come to earth to declare Him (John 1:18). Moreover, as they lived on the other side of the Cross,

1

they knew nothing of the privileges, blessings, and intimate relationships which are unfolded in the Apostolical Epistles. Also, the Holy Spirit had not been given, as a divine favour of love; this could not be until the risen Christ took His seat on high on the ground of accomplished redemption (John 7:39). No doubt, there were from time to time special enduements with the Holy Spirit's power for particular service; but that is not the same thing as the Holy Spirit given to abide with the saints for ever (John 14:16). Thus we are more favoured, and have more at our command, than the prophet who is the theme of this book.

What made Elijah the mighty man he was? Prayer *preceded by deep exercise concerning the condition of things around him.* He walked in conscious dependence upon God. He was his strength and stay. This surely is open to believers in any age. Sometimes we excuse our non-success in service by saying, "it is a day of small things" (Zech: 4:10). Another has suggested that we had far better say, "it is a day of small men!" But why should we be small men? Why should we not be filled with zeal for the glory of God, as Elijah was? Our work will, of course, differ from his in character. Every crisis has its own needs, and God knows where to find His suited instruments. But why should not the reader say, "Here am I; send me." (Isa: 6:8).

Elijah the Prophet

NEARLY three thousand years have passed away since Elijah witnessed for God upon earth, but he is by no means a forgotten character. The ear that is divinely alert still hears, as it were, his firm step and stinging words. His stern denunciations of evil caused all classes to tremble before him. In his burning zeal for God; in his righteous indignation against the apostasy of his nation; the prophet was equally bold towards kings, priests, prophets, and people. John the Baptist resembled Elijah in this. The Lord God of Israel, against whom the chosen people were so grievously unfaithful, was a living reality to him. The knowledge of God, and the consciousness of His presence ("before whom I stand") made him bold beyond all others in his day. Meditation upon such a character is a holy stimulus for those who would witness for God and His truth in any age. Never were uncompromising men of the Elijah stamp more needed than in this easy-going complacent Twentieth Century. "Man's day" (I. Cor: 4:3) is rapidly drawing to a close. The judgement of God is fast approaching both for Christendom and the non-professing world. The diabolical character of present-day developments needs to be fearlessly and faithfully exposed.

In some respects Elijah was unique amongst the Old Testament prophets. He was the first to raise a dead person, he passed out of the world without tasting death; he left an immediate successor behind him in Elisha; and he had a moral successor in John the Baptist (Luke 1:17; Matt: 17:12). Moreover, Elijah was sent back to earth with Moses to do honour to the Lord Jesus on the Mount of Transfiguration; and his work is

3

even yet unfinished. His voice will be heard again in the land of Israel (Mal: 4:5).

Do we all understand the meaning of the word "prophet?" The prophets of God did not necessarily predict future events: some did so, notably Isaiah, whose Spirit-given predictions are exceptionally rich and full; but many others such as Elijah dealt exclusively with existing conditions amongst the people. It is a simple rule in Bible study to examine the Holy Spirit's first mention of any matter for we thereby learn its general significance throughout the Book of God. Someone has said: "God graciously hangs up the key just inside the door." We first meet the word "prophet" in Gen: 20:7. It is applied to Abraham! In the teaching of the New Testament two ante-diluvian witnesses Abel and Enoch – are called prophets (Luke 11:50-51; Jude 14). but it is nevertheless true that the first man specially called a prophet in the Old Testament is Abraham.

Let us seek to understand the Holy Spirit's use of the term. Apart from divine guidance, Abraham went down to sojourn in the Philistine city of Gerar. To avert possible danger to himself he said of Sarah, "she is my sister." Abimelech the King attracted by her, took her into his house; but God intervened, saying in a dream, "Restore the man his wife; for he is a prophet, and he shall pray for thee, and thou shalt live." Remarkable, certainly, for the whole story suggests that at that time there was more pious fear of God in the mind of Abimelech the Philistine than in Abraham the Hebrew – "the friend of God." Yet Abraham was a prophet, and possessed intercessory influence such as Abimelech had not! Incidentally we may learn from this that even when our spiritual condition is low, our privileges as saints, priests etc. are not withdrawn from us, although for the time being we are not in enjoyment of them, and are unable to exercise them for the blessing of others.

Abraham neither spoke nor wrote predictive matter, so far as Scripture speaks; although when in normal condition his spiritual vision enabled him to look far ahead, and see with joy the day of Christ (John 8:56). A prophet was simply a man who had the mind of God, and was able to utter it. Thus in Psa: 105:15 other patriarchs are called prophets as well as Abraham. They were men in touch with God and could give forth His mind as no others could in their day.

The words of the woman of Samaria in John 4:19 will help us here. She said to the mysterious stranger who was conversing with her, "Sir, I perceive that thou art a prophet," Yet He had not spoken to her either of future glories or of coming judgements; but His unexpected words concerning her five husbands, and the man with whom she was then living, made her feel that He was speaking to her directly from God. Indeed, He was God manifested in flesh, although she had no sense of this mighty fact at that moment.

There were prophets also in the New Testament (Eph: 2:20, 4:2). There was no resemblance between their ministry and that of such men as Isaiah and Jeremiah. It was not the future that occupied them; it was theirs to give forth the mind of God concerning the new wonderful work in Christianity, the Scriptures being not then complete. We even read in Acts 21:8 of four women – daughters of Philip the evangelist – "who did prophesy." But their service would be rendered in private (I. Cor: 14:34-35).

Of Elijah's antecedents nothing is told us. Concerning his parentage, his age, and his up-bringing nothing is stated, unless his name, which means "Whose God is Jehovah," is meant to indicate a pious father who named his son in faith.) God is silent also concerning other prophets. Of Haggai and Malachi, for example, we know nothing beyond their bare names. But what matters? The object of the Spirit of God is not to occupy us with men, but with the messages they carried, and which will continue to have spiritual value until the world's end. Let us remember this when we have to listen to men speaking in the name of the Lord in the assembly or elsewhere. We may conceivably get something very definite from God, even though but "five words" (1: Cor: 14:19), from a speaker quite unknown to us, and whose attainments may not favourably impress us. Look not at the messenger but at the message. "Quench not the Spirit. Despise not prophesyings; but prove all things, hold fast that which is good." (I Thess: 5:19-21).

Israel's Evil History

ELIJAH'S abrupt appearance in public, with his terrible announcement to King and people, calls for some explanation. Walking boldly into the King's court, he said, "As Jehovah, the God of Israel, liveth, before whom I stand, there shall not be dew nor rain these years, but according to my word" (I. Kings 17:1). What a message from the God who at another time said, "When Israel was a child, then I loved him, and called My son out of Egypt" (Hos: 11:1). What was the meaning of the fearful chastisement, probably without precedent in the world's history, which was thus announced by Elijah? Ahab was apparently stunned by the boldness of the messenger, and the terribleness of the message, for he attempted nothing against Elijah at that moment. Yet Ahab had no scruples about shedding innocent blood! In order to understand the situation, it is necessary to consider how Israel stood in relation to God.

No nation has ever held, or ever will hold, a position in the earth at all comparable to that of Israel. That nation forms the very centre of God's ways both in governing and in blessing. The kings and statesmen of earth do not understand this; hence the futility of all their treaties, with bitter disappointment to millions. Israel ignored; Christ ignored; God ignored! What stability can there be even in the most carefully worked-out plans for the peaceful settlement of the nations?

The divinely appointed place of Israel is described thus: "Jehovah shall make thee the head, and not the tail, and thou shalt not be beneath, if thou hearken unto the commandments of Jehovah thy God" (Deut: 28:13). When the descendants of Noah, with their diverse languages, scattered abroad, and seized upon lands here and there to where He would require them when Israel came upon the scene. No-one understood this divine working at the time. God may have spoken of it to Abraham and to others; hence the words of Moses when he placed the international position before Israel's tribes shortly before they entered the land of Canaan: "Remember the days of old, consider the years of many generations: ask thy father, and he will show thee; thy elders, and they will tell thee. When the most High divided (or, assigned) to the nations their inheritance, when He separated the sons of Adam, he set the bounds of the people according to the number of the children of Israel:" (Deut: 32:7-8). Men may at any time lay violent hands upon territories that they desire, but only by divine permission can they obtain them. The all-wise

Creator sees some way in which the wrath of man will serve His purpose. There is thus an over-ruling hand which controls the movement of nations, little as men perceive it. This was true in the earliest days, and it is true still.

When the first nations settled down in their lands, they threw off the knowledge of God which they had inherited from Noah and his sons, and then plunged into idolatory. Rom: 1:28 says, "they did not like to retain God in their knowledge." Their conceptions of deity, under the deceptive influence of Satan, sank lower and lower. First, "they changed the glory of the incorruptible God into an image made like to corruptible man"; soon, they set up beasts, then birds, and even creeping things. The worship of the serpent became popular. It was not naked savages who thus plunged deeper and deeper into the abyss of folly; for the ancient kingdoms of Babylon, Assyria, and Egypt (amongst others) possessed much learning. It is impossible for men to rise morally above the level of the gods they worship; accordingly beast-worshippers soon became beastly themselves in practice. Rom: 1:18-32 should be carefully pondered, for it is God's sad description of the depths of vice and folly to which men descended when they turned their backs upon Him. Let moderns beware of their increasing godlessness.

The country whose divinely-given title is "land of Israel, and which God says is "the glory of all lands" (Ezek. 20:6), was occupied by seven other nations when the people of Israel arrived upon its frontiers. The gross corruptions with which those nations filled that land were amply sufficient to deprive them of any decent title to further possession. In Abraham's day the cup of their iniquity was not full (Gen: 15:16); but it was overflowing when Israel's hosts came upon them as

God's executioners. To anyone who doubts the righteousness of dispossessing those nations to make room for Jehovah's chosen people, it is sufficient to quote Lev: 18:25: "the land is defiled: therefore I do visit the iniquity thereof upon it, and the land itself vomiteth out its inhabitants."

The land was promised unconditionally by Jehovah to Abraham, Isaac and Jacob, and in the Kingdom-age their seed will possess it from the Nile to the Euphrates. But in Joshua's day they entered Canaan under the Sinai covenant, on the ground of responsibility. The law's conditional "ifs" became their ruin. When Moses the Mediator finished his course, he left no successor, properly speaking. The High-priest was established as the link between Jehovah and the people, and the civil leader was placed under his guidance. "He shall stand before Eleazer the priest, who shall ask counsel for him after the judgement of Urim before Jehovah: at his word shall they go out, and at his word they shall come in, both he, and all the children of Israel with him" (Num: 27:18-23). When the priesthood became morally corrupt (1. Sam: 2:29-30), God spoke of a king. Leaving aside the disastrous episode of Saul, the people's choice, David was God's appointed king, and the priesthood fell into a secondary position. The Kingdom reached the height of its power and splendour under David and Solomon. These kings were both typical of Christ, the only true hope of Israel and the nations. David typified Him as the man of war, victorious over all His people's foes; and Solomon typified Him as the man of peace. Glory and prosperity unexampled filled the land during Solomon's reign; but, alas! that most gifted monarch became leader of the people in serious departure from God. To gratify his many foreign wives he filled the land with strange gods (1 Kings 11).

When "the God of glory" called Abraham, and revealed to him His thoughts (Acts 7:2) His purpose was to recover and bless all the nations by the instrumentality of his seed (Gen: 12:2-3; 22:18). When Abraham was thus called the whole earth was sunk in the darkness and impurity of idolatory; indeed, Abraham's own family "served other gods" (Josh: 24:2). It was sovereign grace therefore on God's part thus to bless Abraham, and then make him a blessing to others. The kingdom of Israel was established as God's witness in the earth; the people should have faithfully held aloft the lamp of divine truth for the enlightenment of all. When they descended to the level of the nations around them, their testimony was gone, and the blessing of the nations became impossible. It awaits the day of Christ. When He appears in Kingdom-majesty, all that has failed in the hands of Adam, Noah, David, Solomon, and others, He will take up and fulfil gloriously.

The disruption of Israel followed Solomon's death, and the breach has not been healed unto this day. Ten tribes followed the lead of Jeroboam the son of Nebat; the remaining two continued with the house of David. Jehovah promised Jeroboam "a sure house" if he would walk in His ways, for Jeroboam understood that God was disciplining the unfaithful royal house through him; nevertheless, Jeroboam having no faith in God and His Word, and fearing for the security of his throne if the people continued to go up to Jerusalem to worship, installed golden calves in Bethel and Dan, and presumably built sanctuaries for them (1. Kings 11:37-38: 12:.26-30; Amos 7:13). He ordained priests from amongst all classes (ignoring the special privilege of the Levites); and he instituted feasts of his own devising in defiance of Jehovah's law as laid down in Lev: 23. Thus the people were wholly diverted from God's centre, and from His order connected therewith. All this was more

Jeroboam

than unfaithfulness; it was open apostasy.) Happily, considerable numbers abhorred these evils, for the Word of God had some authority over their hearts; they turned their backs upon Jeroboam's evil inventions, in some cases surrendering their homes and lands and they went south where there was still a measure of respect for Jehovah's Word, and where at any rate they could worship in the house that was called by His name. That this large movement was a true spiritual work is clear from the following passage: "out of all the tribes of Israel such as set their hearts to seek Jehovah the God of Israel came to Jerusalem to sacrifice unto Jehovah the God of their fathers." The influence of these pious immigrants was so good that for three years the two tribes "walked in the way of David and Solomon" (2 Chron: 11:13-17). The deplorable break-up of the nation; the report of the wickedness of Jeroboam nd his followers; and the coming amongst them of a crowd of pious souls (leaving their all behind them), apparently woke up Rehoboam and his two loyal tribes to the seriousness off the devilries which had been developing in the land for some years, and for a time (alas, only for a time) things went well.

The movement of these Northerners who desired to continue faithful to Jehovah when the mass became apostate has a message for us today. Israel's history has been "written for our admonition" (1. Cor: 10:11). We who stand in Israel's place in testimony for God in the earth should profit by the Holy Spirit's records. How do matters stand with us at this time? We open our Bibles at the early chapters of the Book of Acts, and we read with delight how Christianity began. What love! What devotedness! What close attachment to the teaching of the Apostles, who were God's mouthpieces for the new regime!

The merest glance at the intervening centuries tells us

that the spiritual decline has been terrific. Unity has been thrown to the winds. Rival "churches", National or otherwise, have arisen; positive idolatry is practised throughout the greater part of Christendom; and even those communities which profess to abhor Greek and Roman superstitions are themselves honeycombed with deadly heresies. The call to separation rings out clearly in the Word of God, notably in 2 Cor: 6:14-18; and 2 Tim: 2:15-26. Do we heed it? But separation, to be acceptable to God, must be thorough and complete. It must enter into all the circumstances of our lives. The great call to religious separation in 2 Cor: 6:14-18 is followed with an earnest appeal to "cleanse ourselves from all filthiness of flesh and spirit, perfecting holiness in the fear of God" (2. Cor: 7:1). This is very far reaching. It is possible to turn resolutely from fellowship with the world in religious matters, and to speak very strongly against conformity thereto, and yet walk unconcernedly with the world in other respects, so deceitful is flesh, even in God's saints! For example, is it consistent to condemn fellowship with unscriptual religious systems, and yet voluntarily seek fellowship in a Co-operative Society? Again, how can we justly blame the Roman "priest" for burning incense before God (he may possibly do it with a good conscience quite ignorantly), if we ourselves burn tobacco before God and before men? Many speak severely (and not too severely) of a "Sunday religion"; let us beware of a mere "Sunday separation!" Our baptism teaches death to sin and the world (Rom: 6); are we prepared for this?

The Israelites who separated themselves from the wickedness of Jeroboam and his followers, and removed into the Kingdom of Judah desired to cleave to Jehovah's ways as written in His Word. The innovations of unsanctified men were abominable in their eyes. Let us imitate their excellent example.

The Rival Captains

IT seems difficult to realize that little more than half a century had passed since the death of Solomon when Elijah came across the Jordan from the wilds of Gilead with his terrible announcement of the coming drought! In order to understand the gravity of that moment, we must keep before us the evil doings of the ten tribes after they broke away from the house of David, and also forsook Jehovah for the gods of the heathen. God bore with much patience the doings of those years, but the time had now come for drastic punishment. Jehovah in His righteous government was constrained to assert Himself in order to bring home to the people the folly of idolatory and the gravity of disobedience to His Word.

After the disruption, the Northern Kingdom continued for about 260 years. Then the Kings of Assyria destroyed it, and deported the people. Nineteen kings in all reigned over the ten tribes; alas, there was not a single good king amongst them although some were admittedly more desperate in wickedness than others! As we examine the history we find frequently the dismal refrain: "he walked in all the way of Jeroboam the son of Nebat, and in his sin wherewith he made Israel to sin." (1. Kings 26:26 etc) The Southern Kingdom outlived the Northern by 130 years. The King of Babylon was the instrument used by God for its extinction. The people were carried away into captivity, "and the land enjoyed her Sabbaths, for as long as she lay desolate, she kept Sabbath, to fulfil threescore and ten years" (2. Chron: 36). Nineteen kings and one queen ruled over the two tribes, several of them as wicked as any who polluted the Northern Kingdom, while other kings, such as Jehoshaphat, Hezekiah, and

Josiah, were really excellent men. The "salt" of these pious leaders preserved the decaying kingdom from ruin for many years. Alas, for the day when Jehovah could no longer permit *any* of Israel's tribes to continue in the land. His righteousness demanded that He should expel them all.

Jeroboam, in spite of his wickedness, was allowed by Jehovah to reign twenty two years. Jehovah had used him for the chastisement of the guilty house of David; but his own evil course, in spite of his knowledge of Solomon's sins, and also of God's encouragement of himself to go well, made it impossible for him to establish a new dynasty. The "sure house" mentioned in 1. Kings 11:38 could not be; for Jeroboam had led the people far away from their God.

Who can God entrust with power but Christ? He who was faithful and obedient in the days of his humiliation will be equally faithful and obedient in the golden Kingdom-age when God will place all things beneath His feet (Heb: 2:8). At the end, "He will deliver up the Kingdom to God, even the Father: when He shall have put down all rule and all authority and power . . . When all things shall be subdued unto Him, then shall the Son also Himself be subject unto Him that did put all things under Him, that God may be all in all" (1. Cor: 15:24-28). Perfect Administrator, seeking the glory of God, and the blessing of all His creatures!

God might use Jeroboam to chastise Solomon and his house; He might use the Kings of Assyria to chastise Jeroboam's subjects; and He might use Nebuchadnezzar to chastise Judah and its kings; but all these in their turn God has been obliged to judge, for these rods of His anger (Isa: 10:5) were no more faithful to God than those against whom He employed them.

Jeroboam's son Nadab reigned two years only. (1.

Kings 15:25). He was then murdered by one of his captains – Baasha – while they were at war with the Philistines, and were besieging Gibbethon. Baasha occupied his blood-stained throne twenty-four years, and he became Jehovah's instrument for the extermination of Jeroboam's vile family. Baasha's son Elah succeeded his father, but was murdered two years later by an officer named Zimri. This man hoped to establish himself in Tirzah – the capital of the ten-tribe kingdom. But another captain – Omri – aspired to the throne, and within a week he captured Tirzah, Zimri perishing in the flames of the royal palace, which he himself set ablaze when he perceived that his cause was hopeless. But even this did not settle the country. Yet another aspirant to the throne appeared – Tibni the son of Ginath. "Then were the people of Israel (i.e. the ten tribes) divided into two parts; half of the people followed Tibni the son of Ginath, to make him King; and half followed Omri. But the people that followed Omri prevailed against the people that followed Tibni the son of Ginath; so Tibni died, and Omri reigned." (1. Kings 16:21-22) Deplorable record! We are speaking, not of pagan nations, but of God's chosen people, for whom He had done great things from Egypt onward, and to whom He had made known His holy will. They were still dear to his heart – "beloved for the father's sake" (Rom. 11:28). At a much later date, Jehovah, when pronouncing judgement upon His people spoke of Israel as "the dearly beloved of My soul" (Jer: 12:7). Israel possessed the Scriptures; no other nation was so privileged. Yet what a story of lawlessness and transgression is written in the Books of the Kings! Ambitious captains – plunderers and murderers, contending for supremacy in God's inheritance, with no though of glorifying Him, nor of doing good to His poor people. Jehovah might well have challenged those ruthless leaders as in Jer. 13:20: "Where is the flock that was given thee, thy beautiful flock?" Yet not a trace of exercise of conscience is discernible in the land concerning this condition of things; none crying out in the anguish of faith: "How long, O Jehovah . . . Help us, O God of our salvation, for the glory of Thy name: and deliver us, and purge away our sins for Thy name's sake" (Psa: 79:5-9). A downward course is always slippery. Let us all beware of the smallest beginning of departure from the revealed will of God. "Hold Thou me up, and I shall be safe and I will have respect unto Thy commandments continually" (Psa: 119:117).

Omri and Ahab

OMRI did not secure the throne of Israel without a long struggle. A comparison of verses 15 and 23 of 1 Kings 16 suggests that the civil war raged four years. Seeing that half the nation preferred Tibni to Omri this is not surprising; but the condition of the country while these unprincipled men were contending must have been pitiful. Only a few years before, probably within the memory of living persons, the twelve tribes of Israel were a united people. They stood high amongst the nations by the goodness of God and their sovereign was receiving the homage of all the kings round about. The country was wealthy and peaceful. Gold was so plentiful that silver was thought nothing of in the days of Solomon (2 Chron: 9:20). Now – they were divided into two mutually antagonistic nations, and two ruthless military leaders were contending for the mastery in the Northern State. Also vast amounts of Solomon's accumulated treasure had been seized and carried away from Jerusalem into Egypt. "How are the mighty fallen!" (2 Sam: 1:27). Truly the consequences of turning away from God and His Word are disastrous! Let us take heed!

Omri waas apparently an able man, as the world speaks, for he brought order out of chaos, and after twelve years, reign he left the throne of the ten tribes unchallenged to his son. He seems to have overhauled the laws of the nation. In Micah 6:16, long after Omri's death, Jehovah complained that "the statues of Omri" were preferred to His holy ordinances. "The statues of Omri are kept, and all the works of the house of Ahab, and ye walk in their counsels; that I should make thee a desolation, and the inhabitants thereof a hissing: therefore ye shall bear the reproach of My people." It is no uncommon thing for the professing people of God to prefer human rules and regulations to the plain teaching of His blessed Word. The Lord Jesus told the religious leaders of His own time: "Full well ye reject the commandment of God that ye may keep your own tradition . . . making the word of God of none effect through your tradition which ye have delivered" (Mark 7:9-13). Since the Lord spake thus, the Scriptures have been completed; the whole revelation of God is in our hands; yet the great majority of souls in Christendom are far more subject to ecclesiastical regulations and human dictation than to the wholesome Word of God!

In the middle of his reign Omri decided to transfer his capital from Tirzah to a preferable site which had attracted his attention. Being a man of military genius, he desired for his seat of government a place of greater strategic value than Tirzah had proved to be when

Zimri endeavoured to hold it. It could not sustain even
a week's siege! (1. Kings 16:18). So he bought the hill
Samaria of Shemer for two talents of silver and built on
the hill and called the name of the city which he built,
after the name of Shemer, owner of the hill, Samaria" (I
Kings 16:24). Such a memorial of his reign would suit
the vanity of Omri, besides making for greater security
in time of war. Although firm rule, and a new up-to-
date Metropolis may be considered desirable things in
men's eyes, it is the moral and spiritual condition that
counts with God; and Omri became a more wicked ruler
than even his bad predecessors. "Omri wrought evil in
the eyes of Jehovah, and did worse than all that were
before him." He continued the worship of Jeorboam's
golden calves, and added fresh devilries of his own
devising. When he died, he was buried in the new city
which he had created on the hill of Shemer. But "there
shall be a resurrection of the dead, both of the just and
unjust" (Acts 24:15).

"Ahab's son reigned in his stead – Ahab the son of
Omri reigned over Israel in Samaria twenty and two
years." The new king exceeded his father and all others
in transgression against Jehovah. "Ahab did more to
provoke Jehovah the God of Israel to anger than all the
kings of Israel that were before him" (I Kings 16:28-
33). Things were thus ripening fast for the heavy stroke
which fell upon the nation with such devastating effects
by the instrumentality of Elijah.

One of the daring evils of Ahab's reign was the
rebuilding of Jericho by Hiel the Bethelite. Indeed,
anything was possible in those dark days. Flesh had
utterly broken loose, and all divine restraint was cast
aside. "In his days did Hiel the Bethelite build Jericho:
he laid the foundation thereof in Abiram his firstborn,
and set up the gates thereof in Segub his youngest son,

according to the word of Jehovah which He spake by
Joshua the son of Nun" (I Kings 16:34) At the time of
the conquest of Canaan by the people of Israel, Jericho
was the first city to oppose their progess. It typifies the
world as that which would hinder the Christian enjoying
his present heavenly portion in Jesus Christ. Jericho's
walls fell flat by direct divine action, and the wicked
city was given to the flames. Joshua pronounced the
curse of God upon anyone who should venture to
rebuild it, and Joshua charged them with an oath at that
time (R.V.) saying "Cursed be the man before Jehovah,
that riseth up and buildeth this city Jericho: he shall lay
the foundation thereof in his first-born, and in his
youngest son he shall set up the gates of it" (Josh: 6:26).
Five hundred years elapsed between Joshua and Ahab;
but, during all that time, when the people of Israel
frequently turned aside into paths of disobedience no-
one was bold enough to brave the divine imprecation.
Its terms were serious; the daring builder, whoever he
might be, would pay the penalty of his impiety in the
death of his firstborn son at the beginning of his
undertaking, and in the death of his youngest at its
completion. In Ahab's day Hiel the Bethelite was
sufficiently infidel to dare the Almighty in this matter;
but it happened to him "according to the word of
Jehovah which He spake by Joshua the son of Nun."
Abiram his firstborn died when he laid the foundation,
and Segub his youngest died when he set up Jericho's
gates. Truly, "God is not mocked!" (Gal: 6:7).

A form of evil is suggested in Hiel's open defiance of
God which has become painfully common in our day.
The judgements of God are openly challenged; from
many modern pulpits eternal punishment is never
mentioned; and multitudes say impudently that they do
not believe in Hell. We cannot but recall Satan's first

move against our race. Adam and his wife were placed by the generous Creator in a garden of abundance and delight, with one single prohibition. There was a tree in the midst of the garden of which they must not eat, or the judgement of death would ensue (Gen: 2:17). The serpent approached Eve, as we all know, challenging God's word as to this, saying definitely, "Ye shall not surely die" (Gen: 3:4); but the Word of God stood nevertheless, and so it must ever be. "By one man sin entered into the world, and death by sin; and so death passed upon all men, for that all have sinned" (Rom: 5:12).

Hiel the Bethelite, and his wife with him (if she were living), surely felt the bitterness of beholding both the eldest and youngest of their sons laid low in death. Why not abandon the mad enterprise when Abiram died? Alas, for the stubborness of flesh! Satan was ready enough with some natural explanation of the young man's death, and so let building operations continue to the predicted tragedy. Let all the cavillers in Christendom beware! Whatever Satan and his agents may say, there is a "Hell of fire that never shall be quenched, where their worm dieth not, and the fire is not quenched" (Mark 9:44, 46, 48).

The Holy Spirit notes that Hiel was a *Bethelite*. His hometown had many sacred memories which should have influenced the man's soul. Nearby, Abram pitched his tent and reared his altar when he first entered the land (Gen: 12:8). There he enjoyed manifestations of Jehovah, and listened to His gracious promises of blessings for days yet to come. It was at Bethel that God spoke to Jacob in a dream, and opened out to him the future in a very full way, assuring him of His continued interest in him, even though at that moment his ways were displeasing in His sight. Jacob felt that the spot was the very house of God, although no visible temple stood there. (Gen: 28:11-22). Some years later, when Jacob was suffering at the hands of Laban, he received this precious word in a dream, "I am the God of Bethel, where thou anointedst the pillar" (Gen: 31:13). This was a sweet reminder that amidst all his troubles and vicissitudes he had to do with a faithful God. Still later, after years of wandering, "God said unto Jacob, Arise, go up to Bethel, and dwell there, and make there an altar unto God, that appeared unto thee when thou fleddest from the face of Esau thy brother" (Gen: 35:1). This call exercised Jacob deeply. He became aware of many things in himself and family that did not suit the presence of a holy God. He charged his household to put away all the strange gods that were among them, and to purify themselves, and change their garments. To Jacob's soul, now divinely stirred, it was impossible to take strange gods and other evil things to a spot that was to him the very house of God. The assembly is the house of God today; our exercises should be deep and thorough when we gather together to have to do with God.

When Jacob arrived in Bethel, "he built there an altar, and called the place El-Bethel: because there God appeared unto him when he fled from the face of his brother." Note again how Jacob connected the presence of God with the place. In calling it "El-Bethel," which means "the God of the house of God," he took much higher ground than when he built an altar near Shechem, and called it "El-elohe-Israel," i.e. "God the God of Israel" (Gen: 33:20). Self was the centre of his thoughts when he said the latter, the expression of his trust that God would look after him; but at Bethel he rose to the thought of having to do with God in His own house, and thus everything connected with himself must be in suitability to the holy One who dwelt there.

Hiel might well have learned great lessons from these memories; but his mind was too utterly alienated from God to learn anything. Bethel in his time – horrible to say – was one of the chief seats of idolatory. There stood Jeroboam's golden calf, glaring proof that the early sin of Exod: 32 had never been truly judged. Let us not miss the lesson of these Old Testament records. "They were written aforetime for our learning" (Rom: 15:4). From whence comes the repudiation of God's judgements in our day? From those circles which claim to know God and where the term "house of God" is freely used; in other words it is not so much the non-professing world which speaks against the judgement of God, as the leaders and teachers of those "who profess and call themselves Christians." The results of this widespread denial of the judgement of God are disastrous; morality everywhere declines, and deceived souls glide carelessly down to eternal ruin.

Jezebel

JEZEBEL! One of the most sinister figures in the Word of God! This wicked woman not only wrought incalculable mischief amongst God's chosen earthly people in the days of Elijah's testimony; her name is used by the Holy Spirit in Rev: 2:20 as the symbol of a frightful system of evil which has intruded itself into a more sacred circle than Israel ever was. One of Ahab's many sins was his marriage with idolatrous Jezebel. "It came to pass, as if it had been a light thing for him to walk in the sins of Jeroboam the son of

Nebat, that he took to wife Jezebel the daughter of Ethbaal, king of the Zidonians, and went and served Baal, and worshipped him" (I Kings 16:31). (The Israelites were expressly forbidden to inter-marry with the corrupt nations of Canaan;) "thy daughter shalt thou not give unto his son, nor his daughter shalt thou take unto thy son." The inevitable consequences of disobedience in this respect were divinely stated: "they will turn away thy son from following Me, that they may serve other gods: so will the anger of Jehovah be kindled against you, and destroy thee suddenly" (Deut: 7:3-4). Here there is no suggestion that a God-fearing husband or wife might win for the truth an ungodly partner; the very opposite result is sure. The influence of a woman over a man is considerable; it is of the greatest importance therefore that every one who knows God should be divinely mated. (Many a man besides Ahab has been ruined by a marriage contract entered into in defiance of the Word of God.) A great contrast to Jezebel is found in Abigail. Well might David, after she had restrained him from violence, say, "Blessed be Jehovah the God of Israel, which sent thee this day to meet me, and blessed by thy advice" (I. Sam: 25:32). Happy is the man who in any age and in any land, meets an Abigail!

(Ahab was a weak character; Jezebel was strong and energetic. A most unfortunate combination!) I Kings 21:27 suggests that his whole course might have been different had his wife been an Abigail instead of Jezebel. When Elijah pronounced the divine sentence upon him after the murder of Naboth, we read that "he rent his clothes, and put sackcloth upon his flesh, and fasted, and lay in sackcloth, and went softly." This was excellent; and Jehovah so far relented towards him that the judgement was at least deferred. No man's weakness of character excuses his wickedness; still, God in His pitifulness, does take account of the influences which surround us all. "There was none like unto Ahab, which did sell himself to work wickedness in the sight of Jehovah whom Jezebel his wife stirred up" (I Kings 21:25). But he should never have married the woman!

Idolatry was no new evil amongst God's favoured but faithless people Israel. Their whole course in this respect is traced with much detail in Ezek: 20. In Egypt, before the deliverance, they worshipped the gods around them (ver. 8): they worshipped idols in the wilderness, although perhaps covertly (ver. 13), and they worshipped idols in the land (ver. 28). The worship of Baal in particular is noted in Judges 2:11-13; Gideon was instructed by God to throw down the altar of Baal which his father had erected, and also to cut down the Asherah which stood by it (Judg: 6:25); just before Jephthah was raised up for the people's deliverance, they confessed that they had forsaken God, and served Baalim (Judg: 10:10).

The "Groves" so frequently referred to in the history of Ahab and Elijah were really statues of Ashtoreth. Baal seems to have represented the sun, and Ashtoreth the moon. In the divine indictment of the Northern Kingdom, when the people were carried captive into Assyria, we read: "they left all the commandments of Jehovah their God, and made them molten images, two calves, and made an Asherah, and worshipped all the host of heaven, and served Baal" 2 Kings 17:16. Note how "all the host of heaven" is here linked with Baal. In Jer: 7:18 Ashtoreth is called "the queen of heaven." From Job 31:26-27 we gather that homage to the sun and moon was the earliest form of idolatry.

There was a moment in Samuel's day when this evil was apparently sincerely judged. The prophet urged the people to put away the strange gods from amongst them, and prepare their hearts to serve Jehovah only. "Then the children of Israel did put away Baalim and Ashtoreth, and served Jehovah only" (1 Sam: 7:3-4). This was good, for Jehovah is a jealous God, and will not share our hearts with any other (Exod: 20:5; Hos: 10:2). Hence our Lord's rebuke to the tempter in the wilderness, "Thou shalt worship the Lord thy God, and Him only shalt thou serve" (Matt: 4:10). Jezebel's coming to Israel put the worship of Baal and Ashtoreth upon a firm footing. It became the religion of the State, with priests and prophets in abundance who ate at the royal table (1 Kings 18:19). With all this wickedness before us, this gross defiance of all the commandments of God, we can understand somewhat the fiery indignation of Elijah's soul, and the sternness with which be testified against it. Do we feel strongly concerning the widespread disobedience to God and His Word in our own time? Does it turn us to prayer? Does it lead us into complete separation to God, and do we seek courage to protest against it all by the power of the Holy Spirit who dwells within us?

★   ★   ★

It is important that we should transfer our thoughts for a while from the first book of Kings to the Apocalypse. The re-appearance of Jezebel's name in the closing book of the Bible suggests that the gross evils which confronted Elijah long ago confront us also, although in a somewhat different form. Truly, there is nothing new under the sun, and history constantly repeats itself!

The epistles to the seven assemblies in Asia are familiar to all Bible readers. There were doubtless assemblies in the places named, and in each case the message sent was what was needed at that time. Jezebel's name figures in the epistle to Thyatira. The Lord said, "Thou sufferest that woman Jezebel . . . and she teaches" (R.V.). There is a two-fold rebuke in these words, which the Authorized Version obscures. First, there was toleration of a wicked person, in defiance of I. Cor: 5:13; and second, the person – a woman – was allowed to teach contrary to the prohibitions of I Cor: 14:34 and I Tim: 2:12. What a condition of things in the very first century of our era! What early departure from the revealed will of God! The Thyatiran woman called herself a prophetess; i.e., she claimed to teach by divine authority; but her teaching was vile, and intended to lead souls astray. We need not suppose that her name was really Jezebel; the name is used symbolically. On the same principle Jerusalem is called in Rev: 11:8 "spiritually Sodom and Egypt." This means that that which should be the holy city of God will be in the world's final crisis just Sodom and Egypt repeated. The Jezebel of Thyatira, whatever her real name, is just the reproduction of the vile Sidonian princess with whom Elijah had to do.

Thyatira is mentioned twice only in the Scriptures, and in each case a woman's name is connected with the city. But how great the contrast between pious Lydia, who esteemed it an honour to lodge four preachers of the Gospel (Acts 16:15); and Jezebel who sought to deceive Christ's servants who would listen to her and who would fain have destroyed those who refused to listen.

Although the epistles were addressed to assemblies then existing, the fact that they have been accorded a place in a prophetic book suggests that the scope of their teaching goes beyond what was merely local. The number seven is itself significant. From amongst many assemblies in Proconsular Asia these were divinely selected because their varied conditions furnished a prophetic sketch. In Rev: 2 and 3 we have an outline of the extended history of the professing Church from the days of John down to the end. In Ephesus things were orderly, false pretenders (male or female) had no footing there; but love had grown cold. In Smyrna we have persecution; and in Pergamos we find the Church making her home where Satan's throne is; i.e. in the world; Thyatira follows with Jezebel. It does not call for much knowledge of Ecclesiastical History to see in these circumstances a picture of what has actually taken place in the Christian circle. First, love grew cold; then God allowed the flames of persecution in order to revive the affections of His saints; then when persecution ceased early in the fourth century, and the Government began to patronise the Church, worldliness became characteristic; and out of that condition Popery developed, of which the woman Jezebel is the apt symbol.

Here is the Lord's description of the "Christian" Jezebel. "She calleth herself a prophetess, and she teaches and seduces My servants to commit fornication, and to eat things sacrificed to idols. And I gave her space to repent of her fornication, and she repented not" (Rev: 2:20-21). In the religious system which Jezebel represents it is affirmed that "the Church" teaches, and that everyone should obey her voice under pain of eternal judgement. The very principle is false. The Church is never represented in the Scriptures as a teacher at all, but as taught – by the gifts given by the Head for that purpose (Eph: 4:8). Seven times in Rev: 2 and 3 we read, "He that hath an ear, let him hear what the Spirit saith unto the Churches;" therefore, instead of hearkening to the Church, he that would be true to the Lord must hearken to the voice of the Spirit speaking *to* the Church – frequently in terms of censure. The divine voice is heard in the Scriptures, which "are profitable for doctrine, for reproof, for correction, for instruction in righteousness, that the man of God may be perfect, thoroughly furnished unto all good works" (2 Tim: 3:16, 17).

Fornication, as mentioned in the Apocalypse, means worldliness – illicit intercourse with that from which all who fear God and reverence His Word should keep absolutely separate. Rome has always sought the favour of the world's rulers for her own ends; and the rulers have too often paid court to the harlot for some supposed advantage to themselves. The going to and from the Vatican on the part of the professed "Protestant" leaders in recent years has been very noticeable, and nothing but mischief can come out of it. The nations and their rulers in their present grave difficulties need GOD. Trafficking with Jezebel is more likely to deepen than to assuage His displeasure with them all.

Rome's idolatry is notorious. Her images, pictures, shrines, and relics are abundant. The Lord in His mercy has given her ample opportunity to repent of her manifold and long-continued transgressions; but she repents not. Terrible judgements are determined upon the harlot, and upon all her admirers.

From Rev. 2 we must pass briefly to Ch. 17, where we see "Babylon the Great, mother of *the* harlots and the abominations of the earth" riding upon a scarlet coloured beast. This "mystery" woman is the final development of Jezebel, after all true saints have been removed to the Father's house on high. The fact that the woman is show riding upon the beast suggests that the religious power will acquire considerable influence over the governments at the time of the end. But the harlot's supremacy will be short-lived. The infuriated kings will, when the moment is ripe for it, turn upon her, "make her desolate and naked, and shall eat her flesh, and burn her with fire." It is the will of God, little as the kings mean it so (Rev. 17:16-17). This is the end of that which calls itself "the Roman Catholic Church," largely augmented in its last stage by much that is at this moment distinct from it. Ahab's Jezebel had a gruesome end (2 Kings 9:33-37); that which has reproduced her amazing enormities, and practised them in the name of "Him that his holy, Him that is true" (Rev. 3:7) will have a fearful end also. Meantime, God would have all who love His truth stand in stern separation from everything that is even remotely suggestive of Jezebel and Babylon (Rev. 18:4).

Elijah's Prayer

THE presence of a prophet in Israel pre-supposed a condition of failure. Had God's order operated as it should, there would have been no need for special divine intervention. When kingship was established in the person of David (after the complete break-down of the priesthood) Jehovah intended that the king should henceforth be the link between Himself and the people. The king should be His mouthpiece to them. Kingship soon failed spiritually – even the richly-gifted Solomon led the way in idolatry; but God, who is never without resource, raised up prophets from time to time, who delivered His message to the people independently of

B

the king, from whose oppressive hand God's faithful witnesses frequently suffered. What the conditions were in the Northern Kingdom of Israel during several reigns, we have seen; there was indisputably urgent need for a stern witness, and Elijah was the man chosen by God for this service.

The sovereignty of God in His choice of instruments for His work is noticeable throughout the Scriptures. Take the Scriptures themselves: the first writer had the status of an Egyptian prince, "and was mighty in his words and his deeds" (Acts 7:22); the last writer was a Galilean fisherman: and between these two we find kings, priests, prophets, a military commander, a prime minister, a herdman, a tax-gatherer, and a doctor (besides others). We have seen that there was urgent need for a testimony to Israel in Ahab's day yet God did not send an Aaronite priest from Jerusalem, nor a man otherwise notable; His sovereign choice was a simple countryman without any official or social standing, and apparently without literary accomplishments. In the same sovereign way of acting, when God desired to send a peculiarly solemn testimony to Israel in the early days of our era, He did not use an apostle, but took Stephen from his humble service amongst the widows for His purpose (Act 6).

Why did God employ Elijah? His flaming zeal for the glory of God, and his simple-hearted faith in His Word and in His power is the answer. It is interesting to observe that there are two Elijah's noted in the Scriptures, and the contrast between them will help us at this point. The other Elijah is found in Ezra 10:21. He was one of many priests of Aaron's favoured line who sinned against God after His merciful restoration of a Jewish remnant from the captivity in Babylon. In flagrant defiance of the Word of God this man had taken a strange wife. Where was zeal for God's glory in such a one? What sense had he of the blessedness of special relationship of Jehovah? Also, what neglect, or rejection, of the lessons which he should have learned from the disasters which had fallen upon the nation because of their unfaithfulness to God! Thus, the instructed priest of Ezra 10:21 stands out as a model of disobedience to the known will of God. The very mention of him (although we would not ignore his repentance) makes us realize the more the loyalty and zeal of the humble Tishbite.

It was a great moment when Elijah walked into the king's presence with his brief but grave message: "As Jehovah the God of Israel liveth, before whom I stand, there shall not be dew nor rain these years, but according to my word" (I Kings 17:1). What the Lord Jesus said of John the Baptist would have suited Elijah also: "What went ye out to see? A man clothed in delicate raiment? behold, they that wear delicate raiment are in King's houses" (Matt. 11:8). Elijah is described in 2 Kings 1:8 as a man in "a hairy garment, and girt with a girdle of leather about his loins." John the Baptist dressed similarly (Matt. 3:4). In such attire Elijah confronted Ahab and his court. What lay behind this amazing courage? For this we must enquire of the apostle James who wrote about our prophet nearly a thousand years after his day (James 5:17). Elijah was pre-eminently a man of prayer. Being thus accustomed to have dealings with the Sovereign of the universe at His lofty throne he did not dread Israel's petty sovereign sitting upon his throne, whatever might be the strength of the armed guard around him! Elijah's God was a living God; and he lived, served, and testified in the consciousness of His presence.

If any would enquire why Elijah's prayer is not

mentioned in the book of Kings, the answer is that the
Scriptures are one great whole, and it does not always
please God to tell us all that could be told about any
matter in a single book. Every detail has been placed in
its own suited setting by the all-wise Spirit of God.
Thus, in Num. 13 we have Jehovah commanding Moses
to send twelve men to spy out the land of Canaan;
but in Deut. 1 we learn that the people in their unbelief
demanded this. Both statements are true. Reading both
we have God's side and man's side of the matter. In
Deut. 1 we have the record of the people's
unfaithfulness, and in Num. 13 we are reminded of
God's ceaseless interest in them in spite of their unbelief.
Another example will be found in the life of the apostle
Paul. The brethen in Antioch, after there had been
much disputation with teachers who desired to put
Gentile Christians under law, requested Paul and
Barnabas, with some of their own number to go up to
Jerusalem about the question; but in Gal. 2:1, 2 Paul
says, "I went up by revelation". There were thus two
sides to the matter – the brethen's request, and the
Lord's direction.

In I Kings 17 we have Elijah's public action, which
probably startled all who heard it; and in James 5 we
have his private dealings with God before he came forth
into public view. The connection in James's epistle
concerns us intimately; we are all exhorted to pray for
one another, and the Apostle adds, "the ardent and
energetic prayer of the righteous man has great efficacy"
(Darby's Translation). Let no-one miss the seriousness
of this. Every Christian has access to the throne of grace;
but the man who would pray for others must be himself a
righteous man; he must look well to his own conduct,
and examine carefully his own ways, ere he ventures
into the Sanctuary. Even then prayer must not be a

mere utterance of words, the whole spirit of the man must be ("ardent *righteous* and energetic." Here we have the secret of successful prayer.)

Many years ago, a newly-converted Methodist was taken to the prayer-meeting of some special friends of mine. After he had listened to three wordy prayers which told God many things that He knew already, and which asked for nothing in particular, the young man arose, and cried out, "O God, teach these good men how to pray!" The elder brethen were annoyed at the intrusion; but my sympathies are with the young man!

Prayer, to be of any avail, must come from prepared hearts, and be definite and pointed. "Elias was a man of like passions as we are, and he prayed earnestly that it might not rain: and it rained not on the earth by the space of three years and six months. And he prayed again, and the heaven gave rain, and the earth brought forth her fruit" (James 5:17-18).

We must think of Elijah exercised before God in the solitudes of Gilead about the appalling condition of His people. (The prophet's words to Ahab, however unexpected and startling were no mere spasmodic outburst. He had doubtless spent much time before God about the nation and its ways.) He loved the people; he longed to see them right with God; but the grossest evils had become so deeply entrenched, that he felt something drastic was required in order to bring the people to their senses. So he turned to prayer. (Acceptable prayer must be based upon the Word of God, and the prophet doubtless remembered Deut. 11:16, 17:) "Take heed to yourselves, that your heart be not deceived, and ye turn aside, and serve other gods and worship them; and Jehovah's wrath be kindled against you, and He shut up the heaven, that there be no rain, and that the land yield not her fruit; and ye perish quickly from off the good land which Jehovah giveth you." With such words before him, the distressed prophet cried out of the depth of his heart. "O God, stop the rain!" Being fully assured that he had the mind of God about the matter he went into the presence of Ahab, and said, "There shall not be dew or rain these years, but according to my word." God responded to His servant's faith, "and it rained not on the earth by the space of three years and six months."

When the disciples asked the Lord Jesus why they were unable to cast out a demon (although they had been sent forth with divine authority so to do – Luke 9:1), He replied, "Because of your unbelief . . . this kind goeth not out but by prayer and fasting" (Matt. 17:10-21).

Elijah was a man of deep spiritual feeling; in communion with God he felt the evil of the circumstances around him. Are we like Elijah in this respect? The reader would be wise to lay down this book, and read Daniel's ninth chapter throughout. That holy man of God "with fasting, and sack-cloth and ashes" prayed and confessed the sins of his people and their rulers from the very beginning of their national history, and he appealed humbly to God for His mercy. Ezra and Nehemiah prayed on similar lines, each in the ninth chapter of his book. If these Old Testament saints could look back over 900 years of their people's history, and confess their sins as their own, what have we to say concerning 1000 years of disobedience and unfaithfulness in the Church of God? Have we no responsibility concerning what lies behind us? Or are we so enslaved by denominational interests, and by the interests of "local assemblies," that larger thoughts are quite foreign to our minds?

If we would be useful to God in these last days, we

must train our souls to look at things from God's point of view. The deep spiritual feelings of men of old are a rebuke to us, for these are days of shallowness and superficiality. Daniel, when told of judgements yet to come (in Ch. 7 of his book) says "my cogitations much troubled me, and my countenance changed in me"; when further solemn things were made known to him, in his eighth chapter, he says, "I Daniel fainted and was sick certain days"; and in Chap. 10, when in prayer to God about His unhappy people, he mourned three full weeks, he ate no pleasant bread, neither flesh nor wine entered his mouth, nether did he anoint himself. Such deep spiritual exercise is well-pleasing to God; but are we up to it? In the light of what the Spirit has written concerning Elijah, Moses, Samuel, Daniel, Paul, Epaphras, and others, we may well ask ourselves. Have we yet learned how to pray?

The Great Drought

IT delights God as Creator and Governor of the universe, to lavish His bounties upon men, in spite of their unworthiness and ingratitude. "Jehovah is good to all, and His tender mercies are over all His works" (Psa. 165:9). The Lord Jesus, when bidding His disciples to love their enemies, said, "that ye may be the sons of your Father which is in heaven: for He maketh His sun to rise on the evil and on the good, and sendeth rain on the just and on the unjust" (Matt. 5:45). When the foolish pagans of Lystra desired to offer sacrifices to Barnabas and Paul as gods come down to earth in the likeness of men, these faithful men ran in amongst them, and bore testimony to the one true God. Of Him they said, "He left not Himself without witness, in that He did good, and gave you rain from heaven, and fruitful seasons, filling your hearts with food and gladness" (Acts 14:17). The regularity of the seasons, as they come and go, are the abiding evidences of God's gracious interest in His creatures. Faith, perceiving this, cries out: "O Jehovah, how manifold are Thy works! in wisdom hast Thou made them all: the earth is full of Thy riches" (Psa. 105:24). What then does it mean when He forbids showers to fall or the sun to shine?

It was doubtless with a heavy heart that Elijah turned away from the King's palace after the delivery of his heavy message, and went into retirement. He certainly did not desire the ruin of the nation. Had there been prompt repentance, so that the threatened stroke might be averted, his heart would have danced for joy. In this he was unlike Jonah, to whom the repentance of a threatened people was a real annoyance! (Jonah 4:1). It touched his dignity that he should have uttered a sentence which a merciful God did not execute!

What a God is ours! Oh, the grace that He has revealed to us in the Gospel of His Son! The heart of God is filled with joy, and all heaven shares His joy, when even an individual sinner humbles himself in true repentance before Him. Surely we have all tasted the grace that pardons, cleanses, and reconciles – all in virtue of the precious blood of Christ!

Before the children of Israel moved away from Mount Sinai. Jehovah had a plain talk with them about their future. Lev. 26 should be read. "If ye walk in My statues, and keep My commandments, and do them; then I will give you rain in due season and the land shall yield her increase, and the trees of the field shall yield their fruit. And your threshing shall reach unto the vintage, and the vintage shall reach unto the sowing time: and ye shall eat your bread to the full, and dwell in your land safely (10:3-5). This would be prosperity indeed! "But if ye will not hearken unto Me, and will not do all these commandments; and if ye shall despise My statues . . . I will do this unto you . . . I will break the pride of your power: and I will make your heaven as iron, and your earth as brass: and your strength shall be spent in vain; for your land shall not yield her increase, neither shall the trees of the land yield their fruits" (10:14, 16, 19, 20). Nearly forty years later, Jehovah addressed the new generation in similar terms but even more solemnly, and at greater length. Read Deut. 28. Every blessing should be theirs in the land to which they were going, and they would be the envy of the surrounding nations, if they would hearken diligently unto the voice of Jehovah their God, to observe and to do all His commandments (10:1). "But it shall come to pass, if thou wilt not hearken unto the voice of Jehovah thy God, to observe to do all His commandments and His statues . . . thy heaven that is over thy head shall be brass and the earth that is under thee shall be iron" (10:15 24). No words could be plainer. With these words ringing in their ears, as it were, Israel's tribes entered the good land. It is a blessed thing to be in relationship with God, but it is also very solemn. "You only have I known of all the families of the earth: therefore I will punish you for all your inquities" (Amos 3:2). The nearer to God the more severe the discipline. In Elijah's day Jehovah still recognised the people as His own, although they (the ten tribes) no longer recognised Him as their God. Hence the judgement of the great drought, while other nations as idolatrous and vile as Israel, were not smitten thus. So now, "the time is come that judgement must begin at the house of God"

(I Pet.4:17). Those who profess to own the lordship of
Christ are therefore amenable to special divine
discipline. There were doubtless many liars in
Jerusalem in the days of Ananias and Sapphira, but
none was specially singled out for the judgement of
God, but these who knew His will (Acts 5). Many ill-
behaved Corinthians were made sick, and some even
died, while they were almost certainly persons in the
same city (as men would judge) guilty of more and
graver transgressions, yet they were suffered to live!
Solemn thoughts these for us all! But the Apostle adds:
"If we would judge ourselves, we should not be judged.
But when we are judged, we are chastened of the Lord,
that we should not be condemned with the world" (I
Cor. 11:30-32). The world's judgement is sure; every
sin will be remembered; even the secrets of men's hearts
will be laid bare; but from all that the grace of God has
exempted those who believe. Our judgement under His
governing hand, is here and now. (Compare I. Pet.
1:17).

When Solomon led Israel in prayer at the dedication
of the temple, he thought of every kind of trouble which
might come upon the people in the future, including the
stoppage of the rain. "When heaven is shut up, and
there is no rain, because they have sinned against thee;
if they pray towards this place, and confess Thy name,
and turn from their sin because Thou afflictest them;
then hear Thou in heaven, and forgive the sin of Thy
servants and of Thy people Israel, when Thou teachest
them the good way in which they should walk, and give
rain upon Thy land, which Thou hast given to Thy
people for an inheritance" (I Kings 8:35-36). Mark the
words, "if they pray towards this place." Israel did
nothing of the kind in Elijah's day. Their hearts were
stubborn; there was no sense of guilt; and they were in

no mood for humiliations before God. As for His loved centre, they had definitely turned their backs upon it. Bethel and Dan with their golden calves, were more to the taste of Ahab's followers than Zion where Jehovah dwelt in the midst of His people, with the atoning blood ever upon the mercy-seat under His holy eye.

What a contrast between the happy condition of the people in the early days of Solomon's reign and in the reign of Ahab and Jezebel! In Solomon's day "Judah and Israel were many, as the sand is by the sea in multitude, eating and drinking, and making merry" (I Kings 4:20). In Ahab's day, a consuming drought for three years and six months! Who can imagine the conditions of the country, and the privations of the people? It gives God no pleasure to smite the children of men, whoever they may be, nor does it please Him to blight the landscape. The Son of God, when upon earth, said, "Consider the lilies, how they grow; they toil not, they spin not: and yet I say unto you, that Solomon in all his glory was not arrayed like one of these" (Luke 12:27). In His gracious condescension, He could take notice of one of the humblest of flowers, and draw attention to its simple beauty, which, being divine handiwork, was more lovely in His sight than the man-made robes of Israel's wealthiest king. As we write, vast areas in Europe, Asia, and elsewhere are in an appalling condition of devastation as the result of men's sin and folly. If men in their hardness of heart do not feel the grievousness of all this, God does.

Blessed be His name, He will change everything at the appointed hour. The public manifestation of Christ, accompanied by the "many sons," will introduce earth's jubilee. (Rom. 8:19). Then "the wilderness and the solitary place shall be glad, and the desert's shall rejoice and blossom as the rose; it shall blossom abundantly, and rejoice even with joy and singing . . . in the wilderness shall waters break out, and streams in the desert" (Isa. 35:1, 2, 6). "There shall be abundance of corn in the earth upon the top of mountains; the fruit thereof shall shake like Lebanon; and they of the city shall flourish like grass of the earth" (Psa. 72:16).

> Lord, Lord, Thy fair creation groans;
> The earth, the air, the sea,
> In unison with all our hearts,
> And calls aloud for Thee.

> (Sir Edward Denny)

Until He comes, and men with one accord, humbly acknowledge Him, all schemes of reconstruction are in vain. The diligent builders of today will be the mad destroyers of tomorrow! There is a driving force behind men of which they are but little conscious. They speak and write of the futility of war, yet spend time, energy, and wealth in preparation for, and in the prosecution of it! Surely Satan, the malign and astute deceiver and destroyer, laughs at his dupes! Yet the multitudes prefer him to the Christ of God! When our blessed Lord was here, and cast a legion of demons out of a desperate man who was the terror of the district, "the whole multitude of the country of the Gadarenes round about besought Him to depart from them" (Luke 8:37). Apparently not a single voice was raised in gratitude to Him for the immense benefit He had conferred upon the neighbourhood, and none desired Him to remain! This is still the attitude of benighted man – no God, no Christ! Thus slaughter and devastation continue, becoming ever more serious.

★ ★ ★

Not many years after the apostate ten tribes had been carried away into captivity (for they learned no permanent lesson from the heavy divine visitations of Elijah's day) the Southern Kingdom also was smitten with the dearth. How long it continued, we know not. But "Judah mourneth, and the gates thereof languish; they are black unto the ground; and the cry of Jerusalem is gone up. Their nobles have sent their servants to the waters: they came to the pits, and found no water: they returned with their vessels empty" (Jer. 14). The prophet goes on to describe the sufferings of both man and beast. The solemn feature of this infliction is that Jeremiah was forbidden to pray for the people. "Thus saith Jehovah unto his people, they have loved to wander, they have not refrained their feet, therefore Jehovah doth not accept them; He will now remember their iniquity, and visit their sins. Then said Jehovah unto me, "Pray not for this people for their good. When they fast, I will not hear their cry." Jeremiah pleaded on their behalf that their prophets had misled them; but Judah had been as willing to listen to false prophets as their Northern brethren in the days of Ahab. "Then said Jehovah unto me, though Moses and Samuel stood before Me, My mind could not be towards this people: cast them out of my sight, and let them go forth" (Jer. 15:1). Accordingly, all the tribes have been expelled from the good land which Jehovah in grace promised Abraham, Isaac, and Jacob to give them. It is a serious thing to turn away from the voice of God, and to refuse to learn the lessons of His chastening hand. Is the time near when it will be too late to pray for unfaithful Britain – when not even the intercessions of a Moses or a Samuel will avail to avert ruin?

By the Brook Cherith

THE wise man tells us "there is a time to keep silence, and a time to speak" (Eccles. 3:7). Elijah had delivered his message in Ahab's court, and in due course he would speak for God to the nation and its idolatrous priests; in the meantime there was nothing to be said – the time of silence had come. The prophet's experience during his period of inactivity is as instructive to us as all his movements in public service; and we doubt not that Elijah reaped as much blessing in retirement by the brook Cherith as Moses did when he led Jethro's flock to the backside of the desert of Sinai (Exod. 3:1). Moses had been too hasty in his desire to deliver God's people Israel (Exod. 2:11-14). Doubtless during his forty years of quiet shepherd-service he learned the great lesson of dependence upon the wisdom and power of God. Forty years in God's school taught him that God has no use for fleshy energy in the carrying out of His purposes of love. Elijah had not been hasty; but, like Moses, his life was in peril. Both men must be divinely preserved for important services yet to be rendered.

Saul of Tarsus spent a season in Arabia soon after his conversion. When he learned the mighty truth that the despised Jesus is the Son of God, he preached Him in this character in the synagogues of Damascus (Acts 9:20). But he soon went away for a term of quietness in Arabia (Gal. 1:17). The wisdom of this is clear. The Lord's commission to him was very comprehensive in character; his teaching was to reach all classes from the highest to the lowest; and his path would lie through much suffering (Acts 26:16-18; 9:16). What a revolution was being wrought in his life! The bitter antagonist of

Jesus was to be His foremost witness to men! A term of quietness, in which he could revolve these things in his mind in the presence of God, was most desirable. Saul was soon in danger, as Moses and Elijah before him, for the world will not tolerate a faithful witness for God.

The word of Jehovah came to Elijah saying, "Get thee hence, and turn thee eastward, and hide thyself by the brook Cherith, that is before Jordan" (I Kings 17:2-3). We first meet with the formula "the word of Jehovah" in Gen. 15 and there it occurs twice. Abram was being addressed. But whenever God is pleased to speak, He expects to be obeyed.

In every age, the Word of the Lord should alone direct the life of the believer. When Jesus was in the wilderness, and hungry for forty days' abstinence from food, He absolutely refused the tempter's suggestion that He should turn stones into bread. There would be nothing morally wrong in doing so, and He questionably had the power to satisfy His need in that way; but there was something far more important to Him than "the bread that perisheth." It was the Word of God, and He had no direction from Him to do what the tempter suggested. The first man might set aside the Word of God in order to do his own will; the Second Man would perpetrate no such folly. "He answered and said, it is written, Man shall not live by bread alone, but by every word that proceedeth out of the mouth of God" (Matt. 4:4). Here is our perfect example. He lived daily according to this simple principle without wavering. When He came into the world, He said, "I delight to do Thy will; O My God, yea, Thy law is within My heart" (Ps. 40:8). As He moved up and down amongst earth's self-willed millions, He told them: "I came down from heaven, not to do Mine own will, but the will of Him that sent Me" (John 6:38). When the cross lay just before Him, we hear Him saying in the darkness of Gethsemane, "O My Father, if it be possible, let this cup pass from Me; nevertheless, not as I will, but as Thou wilt" (Matt. 26:39). For this perfect obedience the Father loved Him (John 10:17).

The secret of a peaceful life is (not submission to, but) delight in the will of God. It should be to us "the perfect law of liberty" (James 1:25). In response to the mercies of God, we should present our bodies a living sacrifice, holy, acceptable to God. All thought of conformity to this world should be abandoned. We should seek to be transformed by the renewing of our mind, that we may prove by experience "the good, and acceptable, and perfect will of God" (Rom. 12:1-2). If the Word of the Lord really controls us in our private lives, in our business transactions, and in our assembly associations, we shall "walk worthy of the Lord unto all pleasing, being faithful in every good work, and increasing in the knowledge of God" (Col. 1:10). Self-will, and neglect of the Word of God, is responsible for many of our sorrows and mistakes in the various spheres in which we move.

Elijah's obedience to the word of the Lord comes before us in the sacred history, and we feel rebuked as we ponder it; but, wonderful and devoted servant of Jehovah though he was, he broke down utterly when Jezebel's murderous threat reached him, and without any word from Jehovah, he ran for his life (I Kings 19). How much better to have spread out the trouble before God in faith as Hezekiah spread out Rab-shakeh's blasphemous and angry words at a later date! (Isa. 37).

★   ★   ★

At the risk of being thought tedious, it seems

desirable to say a little more about the will of God, and
its bearing upon our lives. Some Christians who appear
to be honest and sincere, nevertheless ask in bewildered
tones how the will of God may be known, for they find
it difficult to ascertain it! None of us need expect God to
speak to us in the same way as He spoke to Elijah. Such
words as, "Hide thyself by the brook Cherith"; "Get
thee to Zarephath"; and "show thyself unto Ahab"
could not possibly be misunderstood. God speaks to us
now in the written Word. We are privileged to hold in
our hands the complete revelation of God; moreover, we
have dwelling within us the Holy Spirit, who delights to
guide willing minds into all truth. So full and complete
are the Scriptures that there is something there to suit
every circumstance in which any saint may be found at
any time. But we must be at home in the book of God,
or obviously we shall be at a serious disadvantage in the
hour of need. The blessed Lord Jesus, when tempted by
the Devil, knew exactly where to put His finger upon
the three passages in the book of Deuteronomy that
suited His purpose. But in seeking guidance from God
through the Scriptures we need not look for such
injunctions as "Thou shalt not go to London on
Monday," or "Thou shalt not smoke," or "Thou shalt
not join a Co-operative Society." God does not deal with
us as though we were infants; but rather as intelligent
persons, standing before Him in the dignity of sonship
and endued with the Holy Spirit. In many matters there
are indeed plain commandments, and the Lord Jesus
says, "He that hath My commandments and keepeth
them, he it is that loveth Me" (John 14:21); but much
more frequently we learn the mind of God from the
great principles of truth which we have pondered, and
stored up in our affection Every department of
Scripture truth – typical, historical, prophetical –

contains important principles which are of immense value to the soul that desires to be altogether for God's pleasure in an evil world. Hence our Lord's words in John 14:23. "If a man love Me, he will keep My words". This goes far beyond keeping His commandments. A simple illustration may help here: – a child who truly loves his parents, and delights in their company, will know instinctively what will please them without being told in specific terms. In like manner, if we are walking humbly with God, with flesh judged, and with one simple desire, to know His will and to do it, the whole path will be clear. When our Lord declared His intention of going into Judaea when Lazarus died, the disciples expressed their surprise, because they knew that there was conspiracy there against Him; but He replied, "Are there not twelve hours in the day? If any man walk in the day, he stumbleth not, because he seeth the light of this world. But if a man walk in the night he stumbleth, because there is no light in him" (John 11:9-10). Having but one desire before Him – to do the Father's will, He did nothing for two days after He heard of the sickness of His friend; but having learned the Father's will, he went forward unhesitatingly. Practically, He was walking in broad daylight, and thus every step was clear. So will it be with us if we "walk as He walked" (I John 2:6).

When we seek guidance from God about any matter, and He delays to give it, let us remain where we are and do nothing, as the Lord Jesus did in John 11:6. The opposite of this is seen in the Jewish captains who asked Jeremiah to seek guidance for them from Jehovah when they had already made up their minds to go down into Egypt. This story of flagrant hypocrisy is written in Jer. 42, and should be read carefully by everyone.

Elijah's experience should be a real help to true
hearts. He went to Cherith by the word of the Lord,
and there he remained until he received further
instructions. The water of the brook became less and
less as the days passed and the drought continued; but
he waited, in faith, assured that the One who sent him
there had not forgotten him. In due time a fresh word
came, and he moved away to Zarephath. Elijah's God is
our God; but with this difference – we know Him as
Elijah could not know Him; to us He is Father,
blessedly revealed as such in the Son of His love. Let us
trust Him fully.

★   ★   ★

We must linger a little longer by the brook Cherith,
and examine yet further Jehovah's dealings with His
servant. Note the words, "I have commanded the ravens
to feed thee there." This sufficed for every need.
Whatever the conditions around – the unprecedented
barrenness – Elijah would not starve, for no word of
God can ever fall to the ground. The alarm of the
disciples when upon the stormy lake was groundless, for
the Lord had said, "Let us pass over unto the other
side" (Mark 4:35). There could be no doubt about the
issue of the voyage with such a One on board; He had
spoken, therefore "the other side" was sure.
The path of obedience is the path of sufficiency. The
disciples were without food in John 21:5 because they
were acting in self-will. Instead of waiting patiently in
Galilee until the Lord came to them as He had
appointed (Matt. 26:32), Peter said, "I go a-fishing,"
and his companions responded, "We also go with thee."
A whole night of toil yielded nothing but
disappointment. Jehovah's word to Elijah concerning

Cherith was, "I have commanded the ravens to feed thee *there*." He was not left to choose his own hiding-place. Jehovah chose for him, and *there* his need was met. If we are sure we are where the Lord wants us, we need have no fear.

It is interesting to observe in the Bible history how obedient the humblest creatures can be to God in contrast with rebellious man. The milch kine who went straight to Beth-shemesh with the ark of God, although their calves were at home, is an example of this. The pagan Philistines were impressed with it, and they acknowledged the hand of the God of Israel (I Sam, 6). Another example is seen in the untrained colt who willingly bore the Lord Jesus into Jerusalem amidst tumultuous crowds (Luke 19:35). The ravens were carniverous birds, yet they carried bread and flesh to Elijah daily. In Luke 12:24, the Lord Jesus expressly mentioned these unclean creatures as objects of divine care.

How blessed it is to have to do with One who is "Lord of heaven and earth" (Matt. 11:25), and who thus has all things at His command! The food reached Elijah regularly; the same God who provided manna every day for Israel in the wilderness (Exod. 16) sent the ravens to Elijah with "bread and flesh in the morning, and bread and flesh in the evening, and he drank of the brook." Our God loves regularity. Unpunctuality and disorderly ways do not please Him. When the Lord fed five thousand men besides woman and children, He commanded them to sit down "in ranks of hundreds and fifties." (Mark 6:40). If any reader is disposed to be unpunctual and slovenly, these facts should be remembered.

We have to think of Elijah as being lonely for perhaps several months. Those were not days of pocket bibles, nor of magazines, nor of expository works; and we have no reason to believe that the prophet saw a human face for all the time he sojourned at Cherith, but he had GOD! should we be satisfied to have no one to speak to but God? What days and weeks of quiet reflection! What opportunities for prayer, for himself, and for his disobedient and suffering nation! How absolutely were all the discordant sounds of earth excluded!

The times become increasingly restless, and the chidren of God are more of less affected by the influences around them. Newspaper reading, and "listening in" are the settled habits of many, to their spiritual hurt. One shudders to hear a large Conference gathering sing with fervour –

> "Oh the pure delight of a single hour
> Which before Thy throne I spend,
> When I kneel in prayer, and with Thee, my God,
> I commune as friend with friend!"

The question naturally arises. How many of these people have ever spent a single hour at the throne of grace? Yet their words imply that it is their custom to do so! Do they all devote even a few minutes daily to Scripture reading and prayer in the home? Brethren, let us watch against every form of unreality. It is possible to utter grievous falsehoods in the presence of God by means of a Hymn Book!

David wrote in Ps. 4:8: "I will both lay me down in peace, and sleep: for Thou, Jehovah, although in solitude (R.V. margin) makest me dwell in safety." Elijah at Cherith could have said the same; no wild beast or other enemy could harm the lonely man who was there by the word of the Lord, and abiding under His watchful eye.

The Widow of Zarephath

THIS Zidonian woman is one of the outstanding characters in Bible history. Nearly a thousand years after her day the Lord Jesus made public reference to her, without, however, revealing her name. But her name is as well known in heaven as that of the woman who put her two mites into Jehovah's treasury (Luke 21:2). In the coming day of recompence these widows will receive warm divine commendation. The widow of Zarephath will have a prophet's reward for her care of Elijah when his life was in danger (Matt. 10:41). All such deeds are carefully recorded by our appreciative God. Lovers of hospitality are very agreeable to Him; and when the Son of man sits upon the throne of His glory, as in Matt. 25:31-46, He will praise to the uttermost those who have been kind to His needy messengers. What joy it will give to those hospitable folk to hear His voice, and what honour to be commended before the hosts of angels who will surround the throne of the King of Kings on that great day! Earth has witnessed many wonderful sights, but has seen nothing yet to be compared with the majesty described by our Lord Himself in Matt. 25.

It is not given to angels to lodge the servants of their Lord, although they may, and do, care for them in other ways. If we cannot now prepare a meal for the Lord Himself as Martha did, we can perhaps prepare one for some hungry man who seeks to serve Him in the Gospel of His grace. Such messengers are described in 2 Cor. 8:23, as "the glory of Christ." We therefore ought to receive such," writes the Apostle John to his friend Gaius, "that we may be fellow-helpers to the truth" (3 John 8). Dear Christian reader, open your doors wide to those who go forth in the Lord's name, and be assured that He regards loving attentions to them as done to Himself. Do not compel the preacher to say on his return home. "They received me as an angel of God. It never occurred to them that I needed food!"

To return to our Lord's public reference to the widow of Zarephath. When He stood up in the synagogue in Nazareth, and read Isa. 61:1-2, telling the people that this Scripture was being fulfilled amongst them by His presence, they presently said contemptuously, "Is not this Joseph's son?" The Lord warned them that such unbelief would drive the blessing of God elsewhere, and He forthwith reminded them of two notable instances when the blessing of God reached Gentiles to the passing by of the seed of Abraham. Naaman the Syrian was cleansed from his leprosy at a time when there were many lepers in Israel who had not the faith to seek healing from God. Also – and the Lord was very full about this case – "I tell you of a truth, many widows were in Israel in the days of Elias, when the heaven was shut up for three years and six months, when great famine was throughout all the land; but unto none of them was Elias sent, save unto Sarepta, a city of Sidon, unto a woman that was a widow" (Luke 4:25-26). The Lord's way of stating the case suggests that it was a great honour that was put upon the Gentile widow; and the sequel proved that she received rich blessing from the God of Israel in one of the darkest periods of Israel's history. This being true, Elijah has been justly called "the first Apostle to the Gentiles." But our Lord's mention of the widow and of Naaman in the synagogue of Nazareth only aroused the anger of the people, and they forthwith sought to kill Him. The very suggestion that God would take any notice of Gentiles (unless to destroy them) was anathema to them. Even the prophet

Jonah to some extent felt similarly.

Jehovah's instructions to Elijah at this juncture demand careful attention; they were most extraordinary, and Elijah was probably surprised when he received this fresh communication from God. He was waiting patiently at Cherith until the book dried up, confident that Jehovah would remember his need in good time. Here is the fresh word of the Lord to him: "Arise, and get thee to Zarephath, which belongeth to Zidon, and dwell there; behold, I have commanded a widow woman there to sustain thee" (1 Kings 17:9). Our God is not always pleased to explain Himself, but He expects His saints to trust Him. Philip was called away from a great work in Samaria to go down to a desert place (Acts, 8:26). As an obedient servant "he arose and went." It is not that our God resents a humble inquiry from a perplexed messenger. Ananias of Damascus was startled to be told to call upon a man called Saul of Tarsus, and he said: "Lord, I have heard by many of this man, how much evil he hath done to Thy saints at Jerusalem; and here he hath authority from the chief priests to bind all that call on Thy name" (Acts 9:13-14). This was no spirit of rebellion in Ananias; he was just surprised and perplexed, and quite frankly said so to his Lord, who answered him very graciously. What a Lord is ours! What a contrast to the petty tyrants of earth!

Elijah, when he received his instructions from Jehovah, "arose, and went to Zarephath." He asked no questions, and made no difficulties; but surely thoughts arose in his mind! Jehovah expressly said that Zarephath "belonged to Zidon." He was thus sending His servant outside Israel's land for bread! When Abram went down into Egypt in a time of famine, he did wrong, and nothing but trouble came out of it (Gen. 12:10). When Elimelech and Naomi, with their family, went into Moab in another time of famine, they also did wrong, and they all suffered deeply for it (Ruth 1:1-5). On the other hand, when the Shunammite woman with whom Elisha had to do, went with her household into the land of the Philistines when bread was lacking in Israel, she did right, for she had a "thus saith the Lord" for the step that she took (2 Kings 8:1-2).

In Elijah's case, Jehovah was not merely sending him out of Israel's land. He was sending him into the kingdom of Jezebel's father. Israel's calamities throughout Ahab's reign proceeded principally from Zidon. This is the more remarkable when we go back somewhat in Scripture. Zidon – "called great Zidon" – was a part of the promise to Abraham and at the time of Joshua's conquest, was actually allotted to Asher, but Asher never had sufficient faith and energy to extirpate the evils which had their seat there, and take possession of the city. Judges 1 is a miserable chapter of slothfulness and indifference; and Asher is specially mentioned in verses 31 and 32 as having failed to drive the Amorites out of Zidon, and various other cities. (Read also Josh. 11:8 and 19:28). Let us not miss the lesson of Asher's failure. If we do not in faith get the mastery over evils within ourselves, they will acquire terrible influence over us as the years pass.

Moreover, Jehovah said to Elijah, "I have commanded a widow woman to there sustain thee." We are accustomed to think of widows as needy persons who should be compassionately cared for by others. Yet Elijah was deliberately told by his God to place himself under a widow's care. The prophet's national instincts would be against going into a Gentile area; his religious instincts would lead him to abhor a hot-bed of Baal-worship; and his manly instincts would cause him to shrink from being a burden upon a widow! But all who desire to serve the Lord acceptably in any age must of all things <u>learn to be obedient</u>. <u>His servants must go where He sends; do what He bids; and deliver the messages that He gives them.</u> Paul wrought in the spirit of this; and at a time when the dealings of God with him in service were somewhat strange, he said; "Thanks be unto God, who always leadeth us in triumph in Christ, and maketh manifest the savour of His knowledge by us in every place" (2 Cor. 2:14). He felt tht he was just a captive in the Lord's hands, being led hither and thither as seemed good in His sight; but the chains were chains of love, and all the leadings were in perfect wisdom. So long as he was unto God as a sweet savour of Christ, it mattered nothing to him what form the service might take, nor where that service might be rendered. Troas, Corinth – all were alike to him if it was the will of God. But oh, the grace that can transform a ravening wolf into "a sweet savour of Christ!"

> "To God be the glory;
> Great things He hath done!"

The Meal and the Oil

WHEREVER the brook Cherith may have been (and the locality has not been satisfactorily identified), Elijah must have traversed many miles of country roads before he reached Zarephath. He would thus see for himself some of the havoc wrought by the drought. He could not have said with the Psalmist: "the pastures are clothed with flocks; the valleys are also covered over with corn; they shout for joy, they also sing" (Ps. 65:13). Instead, he would see barren fields, leafless trees, and dry water-courses. The prophet might have said with Joel: "how do the beasts groan! the herds of cattle are perplexed, because they have no pasture; yea, the flocks of sheep are made desolate" (Ch. 1:18). As one who loved the people, Elijah could do no other than lament to see such conditions in the land of Jehovah's choice, of which He said a little before the conquest: "it is a land of hills and valleys, and drinketh water of the rain of heaven: a land which Jehovah thy God careth for: the eyes of Jehovah thy God are always upon it, from the beginning of the year even unto the end of the year" (Deut. 11:11-12). But sin always yields bitter consequences. Let us beware lest we fall in some way under the disciplinary hand of God.

As Elijah drew near to Zarephath he would naturally wonder with whom he was to lodge. He had been given no address, and there were probably many widows in the place! How should he find the right one? Presently, he saw a woman gathering sticks. Did he speak to God in silent prayer as Nehemiah did? (Neh. 2:4). This is a holy habit that we should all cultivate at every stage of our wildernesss journey. (A beautiful example of pious exercise will be found in Gen. 24:42-48). Did Jehovah indicate His will to Elijah as He did to Samuel in the house of Jesse? Samuel was sent there to anoint a king over Israel. All Jesse's five sons passed before him, but the prophet had to say, "Jehovah hath not chosen these", then, when the unthought-of David was fetched in from the fields, Jehovah said, "Arise, anoint him, for this is he" (1 Sam 16:1-12).

When Elijah found himself face to face with the widow of whom Jehovah had told him, he asked her for a drink of water, much in the same way as the Lord Jesus asked a drink from the woman of Samaria. As the widow turned to fetch it, he said, "Bring me, I pray thee, a morsel of bread in thine hand." This request brought out the woman's destitute condition. She said, "As Jehovah thy God liveth, I have not a cake, but a handful of meal in a barrel, and a little oil in a cruse; and, behold, I am gathering two sticks, that I may go in and dress it for me and my son, that we may eat it, and die" (1 Kings 17:12). Truly, a pitiful story! It will be observed that she brought in the name of Jehovah. This is wonderful! While the foolish people of Israel were turning their backs upon the one true God, preferring the false gods of the Zidonians, we have a woman who, in spite of the unholy influences around her, believed that Israel's Jehovah was the true God. In this she reminds us of Rahab (Josh. 2:9-11). It is important to remind ourselves that, although God has never at any time entered into covenant-relationship with any nation but Israel, He has always had true saints (individual) elsewhere. Peter was constrained to acknowledge this as he entered into the house of Cornelius (Acts 10:34-35). But the widow's faith at the time of Elijah's arrival was very low. She did not say "*my* God," as Paul in Phil. 4:19. Her heart was indeed towards Jehovah (no other

God had any place with her); but possibly she felt that He had quite forgotten her! (Her language was that of despair; she was about to make her last cake; then she and her son would lie down and die!)

When God's governmental hand lies upon any nation, His own saints have to share, at least in measure, the circumstances of the ungodly, whose evil has brought down the stroke; but God's saints may always have the sweet assurance that He cares for them, that His eye is upon every one, and He will not suffer any of His children to be tried beyond what they are able (1 Cor. 10:13). Thus, while others perhaps writhe and even curse under the hand of God, His own exercised children learn valuable lessons, and get much blessing out of adversity.

(How true is the saying, "Man's extremity is God's opportunity!" Great blessings were now to be enjoyed in the widow's home. She will remember throughout Eternity Jehovah's dealings with her, and the story of those dealings has been a stimulus to the faith of God's saints for well-nigh three thousand years.)

(Elijah said to her: "Fear not (oh, how blessed are God's 'Fear-nots!'): go and do as thou hast said; but make me thereof a little cake first, and bring it unto me, and after make for thee and for thy son." If the prophet had said no more than this, his words would have sounded heartlesss and selfish. With only enough meal left to make one cake, he asked her to make him one first! (The word "first" should, of course, be noted. Elijah stood before the woman as the representative of the Great God, and his request really meant that she was to put God first, even at this grave crisis in her life. The Lord Jesus taught this in Matt. 6:33;) and when a man once asked Him to let him "first" go and bury his father. He rebuked such an attitude towards His call

(Luke 9:59). God *must* stand first with every one of us, and where He has His rightful place in the affections and lives of His saints, blessing is sure.

Now let us examine what Elijah's apparently strange request was founded upon. He gave the poor widow a direct and definite message from God. "Thus saith Jehovah, the God of Israel, the meal in the barrel shall not waste, neither shall the oil in the cruse fail, until the day that Jehovah sendeth rain upon the earth" (1 Kings 17:14). He who pledged Jehovah for judgement with Ahab, now pledged Him for blessing with the widow. Her flagging faith promptly responded, "and she went and did according to the saying of Elijah"; i.e. she made first a cake for him; and then found to her delight that there was sufficient meal in the barrel to make another cake for herself and for her son. She found God true to His word, and for a whole year the household of three was thus divinely fed. We need not suppose that either the barrel or the cruse filled up. She would probably be always working on the bottom; but day after day there was sufficiency for them all.

On the principle of Heb. 13:5-6 we are entitled to build our own expectations upon the word of Jehovah to the widow of Zarephath. In Heb. 13:5, the writer quotes words addressed to Joshua (Ch. 1:5). "I will never leave thee, nor forsake thee", hands them on, as it were to us; and then encourages the Christian to boldly say, "the Lord is my helper, and I will not fear what man shall do unto me," He who was faithful to Joshua, the military commander with great responsibilities resting upon him, and who was faithful to the widow and her child, can be trusted to be faithful to us also.

One verse from God sufficed at Zarephath. Without hesitation the hungry woman acted upon it. She proved God's word true; and it is always true. We must pause here, and take account of ourselves. We have, what the widow had not, the whole Word of God. It is said that in the English Bible there are 31,173 verses. What spiritual wealth! There are messages from God for our souls in every direction; but have we appropriated them? Are we feeding upon faithfulness? (Ps. 37:3 R.V.). Saints of earlier ages really put us to shame. They had so few words from God; but how much they were to them! The whole of Ps. 119 might well be pondered in proof of this. The widow of Zarephath gave her all on the strength of one verse from God; Abram in Gen. 15:5 built all his hopes on five words from God – "so shall thy seed be"; Matthew surrendered all on the authority of two words "Follow Me" – from the lips of the Lord Jesus; and Peter risked his life at the sound of one word – "Come" – from the same blessed lips. (Matt. 9:9, 14:29). Peter jumped out of the boat, and walked upon the sea, feeling that he would be as safe there as on the fish quay in Capernaum; and he would never have even begun to sink had he not turned his eyes away from the Lord, and looked at the wind and the waves. How painfully we limit our God! It is true that He is able to do "exceeding abundantly above all we ask or think"; but let no reader of these pages follow the bad example of careless persons who intrude a "can" into the middle of Eph. 3:20. We *can* ask larger things than we do ask, and we could think higher thoughts than we do think, if only our faith were more simple and active. But while all this is true, we must be careful to take note of dispensational distinctions in our handling of the Word of God. As a heavenly people, we must not apply to ourselves words than can only properly apply to an earthly people. For example in Ps. 37:11, we read: "the meek shall inherit the earth." This blessing is true for a faithful Israelite, but no follower of Christ in His rejection need expect to become a great landowner if he cultivates meekness for it simply won't happen!

We may picture to ourselves a happy contented household in Zarephath. The meal and the oil failed not, and the woman and her son had the benefit of Elijah's profitable conversations and of his prayers. There was no home on earth more divinely favoured at that time. The food is suggestive of that which nourishes the souls of the saints today; the meal speaks of Christ, and the oil of the Holy Spirit. The Spirit's ministry of Christ through the written word keeps God's saints well nourished and happy in the midst of a discontented and unhappy world.

Dear Christian readers, do not neglect your food – your spiritual food. Let your very countenances show, as in the case of Daniel and his three friends, that the will of God is good, and that its results are satisfying. Let it be clear and unmistakeable that those who walk with God have an infinitely better portion than those who love the present world.

"Until the Day"

THE household in Zarephath was sustained by the temporal mercies of God, which never failed; but also their hearts were sustained by the hope which He set before them. Let us look again at the message of Jehovah to the widow: "Thus saith Jehovah, the God of Israel, the meal in the barrel shall not waste, neither shall the oil in the cruse fail, until the day that Jehovah sendeth rain upon the earth" (1 Kings 17:14). Mark the words, "until the day" – words from the very heart of a faithful God, who would give deliverance and blessing in His season. The fields were not always to be scorched, nor the trees fruitless, not the streams dry. It was Jehovah's gracious intention to reverse the disastrous conditions, and grant once more a happy blend of sunshine and showers which would make "the field joyful and all that is therein" (Ps. 96:12). However unbelieving might be the multitudes around them, the little group in the cottage would cherish the words of God, and wait in faith for Him to act in goodness by His almighty power.

What a picture we have here of our own position today as believers in the Lord Jesus! The world is in a sorry plight; vast regions have been blighted by the ravages of war; and famine and pestilence deepen the misery. The conditions are beyond the wisdom and power of man to correct; and yet there is HOPE. In God's word – in both Old and New Testaments – we meet frequently with the words "the day." The context in almost every case will show that this gave confidence and strength to men of faith, both in Israel and in the Church. What is meant by "the day?" It refers to a point of time to which God has been looking forward through the ages when He will publicly intervene in the affairs of earth, and clear away everything that is offensive in His sight, and which has brought suffering to both man and beast.

We who believe in the Lord Jesus is this dispensation belong to the heavens – there our portion lies, and we look to see the Saviour as the Bright Morning Star before He shines forth in majesty as the Sun of Righteousness. Everyone will see the Sun ("every eye shall see him"); but only His waiting saints will see the Morning Star. We belong in spirit to the day now – "we are all sons of the light, and sons of the day; we are not

C

of the night, nor of darkness" (1 Thess. 5:5).

All that we see and hear around us which is so displeasing to God is also displeasing to us, for we have been born anew, and also have the Holy Spirit dwelling with us. We feel that we are living and moving in an uncongenial atmosphere; but our hearts nevertheless go out towards men in all their sorrows, and we are glad to be assured by the Holy Spirit that "the creation shall be delivered from the bondage of corruption into the liberty and glory of the children of God" (Rom. 8:21).

"The day so frequently referred to in Scripture does not mean a period of twenty-four hours. It covers the entire period of God's suppression of evil in order that He may establish peace and blessing. The heavenly places will first be cleared of rebels; we learn this from Isa. 24:21, and Rev. 12:7-12; the clearance of earth will follow.

When God sent drought into Egypt He laid His whole plan before Joseph in advance. This Joseph communicated to Pharaoh. There were to be seven years before the seven years of drought. The pagan king was thus made to feel that the God of heaven was greater than all the gods of Egypt. They could neither foretell the circumstances, nor provide for them when they came (Gen. 41). But it did not please Jehovah to tell Elijah and the widow when the longed-for day would dawn. They waited in faith for Him to fulfil His word, and they were not disappointed. In God's gracious time everything around them would smile once more. Meanwhile, His "until the day" would ring in their ears, and rejoice their hearts. God's "untils" should be noted as we read the Word, for they suggest hope. He who has alll things at His command tolerates evil "until." Read Rom. 11:25: Isa. 32:15.

God has not been pleased to tell us when the greatest

of all days will open – the turning-point in the history of man and the earth; but we hear the Holy Spirit's words: "The night is far spent, and the day is at hand" (Rom. 13:12). All God's ways from the moment sin came into the world have been leading onward to "the day" of which we speak. The Man of God's purpose will act for Him, and He will do the will of God perfectly. Chaps. 24-27 of the book of Isaiah have been called "Isaiah's little Apocalypse." It would do every reader good to lay down this book for an hour, and read those four chapters carefully. They speak of sorrow and judgements yet to come upon Israel and the nations, but they also speak of the healthy exercises of faith through which godly ones will pass, whose hope is in God, and who long for "the day".

Politicians may promise their people "a new and better world"; and they may be quite sincere in what they say; but the true remedy for all the ills of creation is in the hands of the Lord Jesus Christ. When He shines forth in glory, and all His saints with Him (all sinners saved by grace), Satan's malign rule over men will end, and the will of God will be done on earth as it is done in heaven. In the light of "the day", which will bring recompense and honour to all who serve loyally now, let us watch our steps, and labour with godly care; "for the day will declare" what manner of servants we have been here for God (1 Cor. 3:13).

"Hope of our hearts, O Lord, appear,
Thou glorious Star of day!
Shine forth, and chase the dreary night,
With all our tears, away!
(Sir Edward Denny).

The God of Resurrection

AFTER some time, a dark cloud gathered over the home in Zarephath where God's goodness was daily experienced, where His word was honoured, and where doubtless the voice of prayer was daily heard. The only child of the woman fell sick and died! It was not a sudden death, thus there were days of deep anxiety for both the mother and her prophet-guest. Remarkably, it was the only son of a widow whom the Lord Jesus raised at the gate of Nain (Luke 7:12): it was an only child whom He raised in the house of Jairus (Luke 8:42); and it was an only brother whom He called out of the tomb in Bethany (John 11). This character of visitation which seems to empty the home of its choicest, is always particularly painful; but while we remain here sickness and death are never very far away from God's saints as well as from others. When the Lord Jesus returns, everything will be changed. Martha was quite right when she said, "Lord, if Thou hadst been here, my brother had not died" (John 2:21). Death cannot subsist in His presence. He is death's master. How blessed is the Christian hope! "Behold, I show you a mystery," says the Apostle in 1 Cor 15:51. This means that he was about to tell his readers something which had never been told before. "We shall not all sleep, but we shall all be changed, in a moment, in the twinkling of an eye, at the last trump; for the trumpet shall sound, and the dead shall be raised incorruptible, and we shall be changed." Then "death will be swallowed up in victory," and in the light of this hope, we can send forth the double challenge: "O death, where is thy sting? O death (*not* "O grave"), where is thy victory?"

The Lord Jesus set before Martha the power that

resides in His person: "I am the Resurrection and the Life: he that believeth in Me, though he were dead, yet shall he live: and he that liveth and believeth in Me, shall never die" (John 11:25, 26). Whether the sorrowing woman to whom He addressed Himself understood Him or not, in the light of such a revelation as that in 1 Cor. 15. His meaning is blessedly clear. As the Resurrection, He will raise all His sleeping saints at His descent into the air; and as the Life, He will change the mortal and corruptible bodies of His living ones, and will make them like His own body of glory (Phil. 3: 22). These latter will never die at all. Rom. 8:11 speaks of those whom the Lord will find at His return waiting for His coming: "if the Spirit of Him that raised up Jesus from the dead dwell in you, He that raised up Christ from the dead shall also quicken your mortal bodies because of His Spirit that dwelleth in you." From this wonderful passage we learn that one reason why believers will be changed at the Lord's coming is that our mortal bodies are the very habitation of the Holy Spirit. Thus they have a sacred character in the eyes of God. Death should not be an object of dread to the Christian; but it wore a different aspect to the saints who lived prior to our Lord's great victory. "Through fear of death they were all their lifetime subject to bondage" (Heb. 2:15). Our position differs from theirs in that we are able to look back at the empty sepulchre of the Son of God, and then look up to the throne and behold Him seated there, crowned with glory and honour. To John in Patmos, the Lord said, with His right hand laid upon His trembling servant: "Fear not; I am the First and the Last and the Living One; and I became dead; and behold, I am living to the ages of ages, and have the keys of death and hades" (Rev. 1:17-18 – Darby's Translation). Having to do with such a

One, we are consciously on the side of victory. "Death is yours," wrote the Apostle exultingly to the Corinthians (1 Cor. 3:22); and to the Romans he wrote that nothing can separate us from the love of God, not even death! (Rom. 8:38).

The home of Zarephath was probably quiet and peaceful for many weeks. There were sufficiency there, and a sense of Jehovah's special interest and care. Then suddenly the cloud arose. Sickness entered the home, which terminated in the death of the widow's only child. How many homes of believers in the Lord Jesus have had the same painful experience! How often have we said at the throne of grace, "Lord, behold, he whom Thou lovest is sick"; then perhaps later we have been constrained to say through our tears, "Lord, if Thou hadst been here –!"

Sickness and death are frequently used by the Lord in a disciplinary way; and perhaps these things have more frequently this character than our dull hearts realize. Certainly, some of the Corinthian saints experienced this; their careless ways brought down the hand of the Lord upon them. "For this cause many are weak and sickly among you, and many sleep" (I Cor. 11:30). These things being true we need spiritual discernment in praying for a sick fellow-Christian. "If any man see his brother sin a sin which is not unto death, he shall ask, and He shall give life for them that sin not unto death. There is sin unto death: I do not say that he should pray for it. All unrighteousness is sin; and there is sin not unto death" (I John 5:16-17). Sometimes perplexed souls ask, "what is the particular sin that is unto death?" No particular sin at all. Two brethren possibly may err in the same way; yet the Lord, taking into account all the circumstances, may lay one upon a sick bed, and take the other out of the world. There is no question of the salvation of the soul in these dealings; it is divine chastening. But "if we would judge ourselves, we should not be judged. But when we are judged, we are chastened of the Lord, that we should not be condemned with the world" (I Cor. 11:31-32). The latter would be eternal damnation, which can never be the portion of even the most faulty believer in the Lord Jesus.

We need to exercise ourselves more than perhaps we do with reference to sickness. We are too ready when trouble comes, to send for the physician; and also when a fellow-Christian falls sick, to ask the Lord to heal him. Should we not, first, exercise our hearts and consciences before God, and enquire of Him why these things have come about? There are sometimes moral reasons why we or our loved ones are laid low. The affliction may be preventive in character, as in the case of Job, or it may be corrective. In any case, exercise of heart and conscience before God is good and cannot fail to yield blessed results. Another has said: "As long as life flows quietly, and our daily needs are met, we may live with little exercise as to much that, in God's sight, calls for self-judgement. But under the exercise of some special trial, conscience becomes active, the vision is cleared, and much that may have been wrong in the past in thoughts, words, habits and ways, is seen, dealt with, and judged in God's presence."

This exactly describes what happened at Zarephath. The stricken mother seemed to recognise at one that the hand of God was in the sickness and death of her child. "She said unto Elijah, what have I to do with thee, O thou man of God? Art thou come unto me to call my sin to remembrance, and to slay my son?" (I King 17-18). Zarephath means "smelting furnace"; the woman was now experiencing its heat; but, like Shadrach, Meshach, and Abednego, who only got rid of encumbrances (bands) in the fire, (this woman emerged from the affliction a happier soul, and with a fuller knowledge of God.) There was evidently something in her past life, or in her innermost soul at that very moment which she was seeking to cover, but God in His goodness to her brought it out into the light in His own way.

"When through fiery trials thy pathway shall lie,
My grace, all-sufficient, shall be thy supply:
The flame shall not hurt thee: I only design
Thy dross to consume, and thy gold to refine."

G. Keith

Elijah felt the position. He realized that his coming into the house had something to do with this blow. He said to the mother, "Give me thy son. And he took him out of her bosom, and carried him up into an upper chamber, where he abode, and laid him upon his own bed." (There is a suggestion of tender feeling in his prayer to God. This stern man, who could face an angry king and a wicked nation, and pronounce sentence of judgement, felt deeply for this poor woman whom he had come to know, and whose heart was now very sore.) The prophet spoke to Jehovah twice. In his first utterance, in which we think we discern tenderness, he said: "O Jehovah my God, hast Thou also brought evil upon the widow with whom I sojourn, in slaying her son?" (Then he stretched himself upon the child three times, as if he would acknowledge that in himself he was as weak as he who was dead; then he spoke to Jehovah a second time, and we note that both in verses 20 and 21 the Holy Spirit says "he cried unto Jehovah." This word "cried" should never be lightly passed over in our reading of Scripture, for it expresses intense longing.) Thus our Lord, at the Feast of Tabernacles in

Jerusalem, "stood and cried, saying, if any man thirst, let him come unto Me and drink" (John 7:37). How He yearned over needy souls!

Such a prayer as Elijah uttered over the dead child, had probably never ascended to heaven before: "O Jehovah my God, I pray Thee, let this child's soul come into him again". Wonderful! There is no previous record in Scripture of any person, Jew or Gentile, old or young, ever having returned from the dead. Yet the prophet prayed thus! His faith was in advance of Abraham's on Mount Moriah, when he laid Isaac upon the altar "accounting that God was able to raise him up from the dead; from whence also he received him in a figure" (Heb. 11:19). Both Abraham and Elijah believed that nothing was impossible with God, and that even death would present no difficulty to Him, but it was one thing for Abraham to reckon that God could raise a lad from the dead, and quite another for Elijah to ask definitely that this great miracle might be wrought.

Be it observed that Elijah's prayer was brief and definite. Shall we not learn a lesson from this? Do we go to our prayer meetings with something definite before our minds? Or do we attend for mere force of habit (a good habit, admittedly), with minds unexercised and unprepared? If it be so, need we wonder that the dreary round of words to which we sometimes have to listen have no set purpose; and, in consequence, lead nowhere? Prayer is sorely needed, shall we not seek to learn how to pray?

Jehovah heard and answered Elijah's brief prayer, "and the soul of the child came into him again, and he revived." With calm dignity the prophet led the lad down from the upper chamber, and said to the mother, "See thy son liveth." The woman's reply is arresting: "Now by this I know that thou art a man of God, and that the word of Jehovah in thy mouth is truth.") We cannot but compare this with what the Shunammite woman said (to her husband) concerning Elisha: "Behold, now, I perceive that this is a holy man of God which passeth by us continually" (2 Kings 4:9). Elisha had sometimes, in the course of his travels, called at their home for a meal, and his deportment suggested the woman's remarks. But the Shunammite was on higher ground spiritually than the Zidonian in that she discerned in her visitor a man of God before any miracle was wrought; the Zidonian needed a miracle to lead her to that conclusion. But both women are included in God's gallery of witnesses in the words, "through faith . . . women received their dead raised to life again" (Heb. 11:35).

★　　★　　★

We must not leave this subject without reminding ourselves that (we know God specifically as the God of resurrection. He has brought back from amongst the dead our Lord Jesus, "who was delivered from our offences, and was raised again for our justification" (Rom. 4:25). This secures every blessing for those who believe, and it reminds us also that our blessings lie outside this world altogether. We do not know "Christ after the flesh" (2 Cor. 5:16); we know Him as risen and exalted to the right hand of God. God views us as risen with Christ, and would have us set our minds on things above, and not on things on the earth (Col. 3:1-2). Paul the Apostle was so deeply impressed with this that he longed to know "the power of His resurrection" (Phil. 3:10). Probably no one ever knew this more than Paul; still, he longed to get a firmer grip of where the resurrection of Christ had set him that he might be wholly influenced by it day by day.

Obadiah

ELIJAH'S long rest at Zarephath was ended by a call
from Jehovah to show himself to Ahab, because He was
about to send rain upon the earth (I Kings 18:1). When
the prophet told the king that there should be neither
dew nor rain but according to his word, he knew not
how long the drought would continue. That was in the
hands of Jehovah. But the drought was long, "for it
rained not on the earth by the space of three years and
six months" (James 5:17). When the rain at last came, it
was in answer to Elijah's prayer, as in I Kings 18:42.
But matters were now to be brought to an issue.
Jehovah was about to display His power, to the
confusion of Ahab and all his idolatrous prophets. Such
striking miracles, as the calling down fire from heaven
upon the sacrifice on Mount Carmel, and later upon the
captains and their fifties (2 Kings I) were not wrought
in the kingdom of Judah. There Jehovah was still
acknowledged, although some of the Kings were evil
men, and led the people astray; but the prophets who
witnessed there could at least appeal to the Word of
God. In the Northern Kingdom another line was
necessary. The people were in open apostasy; Jehovah
was no longer acknowledged as the God of Israel. This
being so, God who was still interested in His erring
people ("how shall I give thee up, Ephraim? Hos. 11:8)
sometimes put forth His power, thus bringing home to
the people that He is God, and mightier than all the
deities of the heathen. Jehovah was now about to assert
Himself on Mount Carmel, on an occasion that will be
memorable as long as the earth remaineth.
When Elijah set out to find Ahab (no more fearing

71

the wrath of the king than Moses before him (Heb. 11:27), he first met Obadiah, who was governor of the palace. (The Holy Spirit records that "Obadiah feared Jehovah greatly." It is happy to note that this is stated before the story of Obadiah is unfolded. In like manner, the Lord Jesus commended all the good that He could see in the assemblies in Asia before rebuking that which was grievous in His sight (Rev. 2:3). Along this line we are frequently terribly lacking in our dealings with one another. That which is evil, or at least unsatisfactory, becomes so large in our eyes that we quite overlook that which is good in those who displease us. Of Barnabas it is written, years after his failures as in Gal. 2:13 and Acts 15:37: "he was a good man, and full of the Holy Spirit and of faith" (Acts 11:24).

It is written of Obadiah, that he "feared Jehovah greatly." The word "*greatly*" must not escape us; for God always notes degrees in piety or activity of His saints. In Rom. 16:12 we read of Tryphena and Tryphosa who laboured in the Lord, and also of the beloved Persis who laboured *much* in the Lord. In the rebuilding of the wall of Jerusalem after the return from the captivity, it is recorded of some that they "*earnestly* repaired," and of some that they undertook a second piece of work (Neh. 3:20-24). It is encouraging to us to be reminded of these things, and we shall doubtless hear more about them at the Judgement seat of Christ.

There are some important lessons to be learned from the story of Obadiah; but first it may be well to compare him with some of his contemporaries. Elijah and Obadiah were both saints of God; so also were Micaiah the son of Imlah, and Jehoshaphat King of Judah. We shall meet them all in the glory of God ere long, like ourselves, sinners saved by grace. These four men fall into two pairs, thus: – Elijah and Micaiah; Obadiah and Jehoshaphat. The first two were bold and unflinching in

their testimony. Ahab called Elijah "mine enemy" (I
Kings 21:20), and of Micaiah he said, "I hate him" (I
Kings 22:8). It is really a compliment to be disliked by
the wicked. "Woe unto you, when all men speak well of
you! for so did their fathers to the false prophets" (Luke
6:26). Obadiah and Jehoshaphat were the opposite of
Elijah and Micaiah. They were not bold and
unflinching, but weak, and given to compromise for the
sake of advantage. Ahab hated neither of these, for they
were useful to him. The Lord Jesus once said to His
own unbelieving brethren: "the world cannot hate you;
but Me it hateth, because I testify of it that its works are
evil" (John 7:7). The Lord in His prayer to the Father
in John 17 spoke of His disciples as loved by the Father,
but hated by the world. The comfort of the one
strengthens us to endure the painfulness of the other.

Obadiah had never learned the importance of
separation from the world. Have we learned it? Are we
true to our baptism? Do we regard ourselves as dead to
sin and the world by the death of Christ? Have we really
taken up our cross in order to follow in the footsteps of
the One whom the world cast out and crucified? Have
we indeed gone forth "to Him without the camp,
bearing His reproach?" (Luke 11:23: Heb. 13:13).
There was much in Obadiah that was excellent, and the
inspired historian tells us of it. When Ahab sought to
destroy all the prophets of Jehovah, and thus stamp all
divine testimony out of his dominions, Obadiah took a
hundred of them, "and hid them by fifty in a cave, and
fed them with bread and water." He feared Jehovah,
but was too timorous to confess Him. He sympathised
with the hunted prophets, but lacked faith to identify
himself with them in their sufferings. His kindness will
doubtless be rewarded in the day of Christ; but God
would have been better pleased had he stood with His

servant instead of being content to patronise him. Moses forsook the honours and comforts of the king's palace, "choosing rather to suffer affliction with the people of God" (Heb. 11:24-25). Obadiah chose to remain in the palace, and benefit the persecuted from thence. All the professing saints in Asia turned away from Paul when he fell into disgrace with the authorities for Christ's sake (2 Tim. 1:15). How should we stand in days of peril? In 2 Cor. 6 we are definitely charged not to be unequally yoked together with unbelievers, but to come out from among them and be separate; and in Eph. 5:2 we are instructed to "have no fellowship with the unfruitful works of darkness, but rather reprove them." Are we willing to take up a stand which may cost us something?

When Obadiah crossed the path of Elijah, he was not occupied with business for God. The land was doubtless full of stricken hearts; mothers knowing not how to nourish their children; and all in a condition of despair. What precious words of consolation he should have been able to take to them from the heart of God! Instead, he was searching the land for food for animals in order to preserve the royal stud! Ahab said to Obadiah: "Go through the land, to all the fountains of water and to all the torrents, perhaps we may find grass to save the horses and mules alive, so that we may not have to destroy some of our beasts" (I Kings 18:5, Darby). Sorry words from the lips of Israel's king; paltry business for a God-fearing man to engage in! The divine ideal for a king is described in the Spirit-filled words of Asaph in Ps. 78:70-72: "He chose David His servant, and took him from the sheepfolds: from following the ewes great with young he brought him to feed Jacob His people, and Israel His inheritance. So he fed them according to the integrity of his heart; and guided them by the skilfulness of his hands." God's

ideal king is thus neither selfish nor tyrannical; but a
wise shepherd of the people, serving in the
consciousness that the people belong to God, and that
he – the King – is just God's honoured servant in rule.
In this spirit David prayed for the people when
pestilence was raging. He pleaded with Jehovah to spare
the sheep, and punish him instead (2 Sam. 24:17). None
but the Lord Jesus has been perfect in shepherd-rule,
and of Him it is written: "He shall stand and feed [His
flock] in the strength of Jehovah, in the majesty of the
name of Jehovah His God; and they shall abide: for now
shall He be great unto the ends of the earth" (Micah
5:4).

There is not a hint that Ahab cared for the suffering
people, but he was troubled lest he should lose his
horses and mules. So he arranged that he would go in
one direction, and Obadiah in another, and find grass
somewhere, if possible. The position was serious indeed
when the King himself undertook the foraging!

In the pursuit of this humiliating business, Obadiah
met Elijah. Using modern terms, the two men were
brethren; but there was no cordial greeting, as when
Moses met Aaron and kissed him (Exod. 4:27). Obadiah
was troubled, and Elijah was cold and reserved.
Although the one was an exalted Government official,
and the other a humble villager, Obadiah trembled
before Elijah; and indeed he fell upon his face, saying,
"Is it indeed thou, my lord Elijah?" Communion with
God, and obedience to His will imparts moral dignity to
anyone. We see this in Stephen when confronting the
Jewish Sanhedrin; and in Paul when standing before
royalty and political and military leaders in Cæsarea
(Acts 7:26). In each case the prisoner took full
command of the situation! Obadiah lacked this. With all
his honours and high salary, he felt that the man who

stood before him in hairy clothing was his superior. Else, why should he address Elijah as "my lord?"

When the prophet bade him go and tell his master, "Behold, Elijah is here," he was terrified. He feared his very life would be in danger. He poured out a veritable torrent of words to the prophet. First, he spoke of the danger to himself; then he told how Ahab had enquired of every known kingdom and nation concerning Elijah, determined to slay him if he could get hold of him. To mention the hated name to the furious king would stir his devilry to its depths. So Obadiah feared; and, as if begging to be excused carrying such a message, he pleaded his kindness to the prophers. "Was it not told my lord what I did when Jezebel slew the prophets by fifty in a cave, and fed them with bread and water?" It is suggestive of a low spiritual condition when any servant of God makes much of his own work. Paul says a good deal about his own labours and sufferings in 2 Cor. 2. It was the bad condition of things at Corinth that made it necessary, but he calls it "folly," nevertheless. But how wonderfully God works! We should never have known how varied and severe were the sufferings of the apostle, had not the story been wrung from him by the ill-behaved Corinthians. It does one good to read 2 Cor. 2, it is a holy stimulus to our souls; but Paul, and every other true-hearted labourer would infinitely rather speak of Christ – the glories of His person, the perfection of His sacrifice, and the greatness of His triumph – than speak of his own work, and thus seem to be magnifying himself.

Going along with the world is injurious to the soul at all times. Thus, Obadiah feared the wicked Ahab, Elijah did not: he humiliated himself before Elijah instead of greeting him warmly as a valuable witness for God and His truth; and, worse than all, he even hinted that the Holy Spirit might act unworthily! "It shall come to pass as soon as I am gone from thee, that the Spirit of Jehovah shall carry thee whither I know not; and so when I come to tell Ahab, and he cannot find thee, he shall slay me: but I thy servant fear Jehovah from my youth." Elijah was perfectly straight-forward in the path that he was pursuing; he was charged by Jehovah to see Ahab, and he intended to do so. The Holy Spirit, who delights to guide the servants of God, would never lead him to be false to a divine commission.

Elijah's answer to Obadiah sounds like a rebuke. "As Jehovah liveth, before whom I stand, I will surely show myself unto him to-day." Whatever Jehovah might be to Obadiah, He was a living God to the proscribed prophet; and he was standing – i.e. speaking and acting – in the consciousness of His presence.

Obadiah must have been far removed from Elijah's spirit to have been tolerated, and even honoured, for years in the royal circle. He must have kept his lips close sealed concerning his God, or the blood-thirsty Jezebel would have treated him as she treated the prophets. Obadiah could scarcely have said:–

> "I'm not ashamed to own my Lord
> Or to defend His cause."

In Isa. 59:15 we read: "Truth faileth, and he that departeth from evil maketh himself a prey." Obadiah was not quite willing to be a prey. In Jer. 15:19 he who would separate himself from the evil around is assured by God, "thou shalt stand before Me; and if thou know how to take forth the precious from the vile, thou shalt be as My mouth." This is exceedingly precious: – nearness to God, and ability to give utterance to His mind to others. Obadiah, alas, knew nothing of this. What do we know of it?

Obadiah comes upon us in the Scriptures as abruptly as Elijah; but while the one passed off the sacred page abruptly (sixteen verses, and no more!) the other lingers in the minds of the sacred historians, and his service and testimony continue right onward to the great day of the Lord!

★   ★   ★

"God of all grace, mercifully preserve both writer and reader from becoming Obadiahs! The rather help us to become Elijahs, not indeed in fiery judgement, but in holy zeal for Thy glory, and in stern separation from everything contrary to Thy will. Amen."

Prophet and King

WHEN Ahab learned that Elijah was in the neighbourhood, he did not hasten towards him with a "firing squad" (or whatever was the equivalent in those days); on the contrary, he approached him with a measure of deference. The wicked king had some sense of the greatness of God whose irresistible power His servant could wield. The whole country was suffering severely under the sentence pronounced by Elijah's lips. The people were proving that it is "an evil thing and bitter" to forsake Jehovah and worship other gods (Jer. 2:19). Ahab's son Ahaziah lacked even the measure of respect and dread that his father had for Elijah. He ventured to defy him and the power of God that was with him (2 Kings 1). But the results were very serious!

Ahab's greeting is very suggestive. "Is it thou, thou troubler of Israel?" (I Kings 18:17 R.V.). We have here a clear illustration of how Satan beclouds the minds and perverts the judgement of men who believe not. There certainly was trouble in Israel; but apparently it did not occur to Ahab's mind to trace it to the idolatry which had spread everywhere. Temples, altars, prophets and priests of an evil character covered the land. There was no disposition either in king or people to get down before Jehovah, and acknowledge the wickedness of all this, with the determination to put it all away. Accordingly, Ahab blamed the servant of God for the widespread distress. Had Satan not blinded his eyes he would have perceived that the fault lay with the king, not with the prophet.

When Paul and Silas went to Philippi there was insurrection against them, and it was said, "these men . . . do exceedingly trouble our city" (Acts 16:20). But "these men" had carried into Philippi the Gospel of the Grace of God; they were telling men and women who were living in the darkness of Heathenism, and who were hastening to perdition, of the Saviour who died for the ungodly. They were putting immense blessings in the way of the people – all "without money and without price." They were proclaiming the true and only remedy for all creature ills. Those who received their words would become supremely happy, even as Paul himself was when he wrote his Epistle to the Philippians a few years later. No truer friends of the people ever visited the city, yet the preachers were charged before the magistrates with being troublers, and were forthwith flogged, and cast into prison!

At every period faithful witnesses for God and His truth are regarded as troublers. Men and women who are all wrong with God do not care to have *facts* set before them. They prefer to live undisturbed in a dreamland of their own. He who pressed upon their attention the gravity of sin, and the reality of God's judgement of sin is a troubler. He disturbs their false peace and spoils their pleasures. Felix cut short his conversation with Paul when his words become very pointed (Acts 24:25). Yet no true preacher would speak only of sin and judgement; he would delight to go further, and tell of the one Mediator between God and men, who gave Himself a ransom for all (I Tim 2:5-6).

Elijah, with divine bluntness, put the truth before the king. "I have not troubled Israel; but thou, and thy father's house, in that ye have forsaken the commandments of Jehovah, and thou has followed Baalim." Men who are willing to rebuke sin in high places are scarce. Nathan dealt faithfully with David (2 Sam. 12); and John the Baptist, every time he found himself in Herod's presence, put his finger upon the fatal spot, saying, "It is not lawful for thee to have thy brother's wife" (Mark 6:18). It is said of the British King Charles 2 – as vile a king as ever disgraced a throne – that he was once offended with a Chaplain for his plain preaching. "I will thank you," said he "to alter your manner of preaching." "So I will your Majesty," replied the Chaplain, "if you will alter your manner of living." This was as it should be. If in our own day there were religious leaders faithful enough to rebuke Dictators and others who are leading millions to ruin, how good it would be! It is, alas! too frequently the habit of professional clergy to accommodate their words to the wishes of the ruling powers. They thus become instruments in their hands for deceiving the people. Solemn thought!

The real trouble in Israel was not Elijah, but Ahab, and Ahab's own conscience must have felt that it was true. The prophet now made a proposal to the king: "Send and gather to me all Israel unto Mount Carmel and the prophets of Baal four hundred and fifty, and the prophets of the groves four hundred, which eat at Jezebel's table" (1 Kings 18:19). Amazing, when we consider the relative position of the two men. Ahab – a powerful despot, with all the military resources of the kingdom at his disposal, backed too by a resolute and ruthless wife; now being virtually commanded by a feeble and friendless individual to convene a meeting of the nation! We have already remarked upon the moral dignity which communion with God imparts; we see it here again in Elijah the Tishbite. The condition of things throughout the country was desperate; it could not continue indefinitely; hence the king consented to Elijah's proposal for a meeting, the outcome of which he could not imagine, but he hoped there would soon be rain!

Prophet and People

SO the great meeting was arranged. "Ahab sent unto all the children of Israel, and gathered the prophets together unto Mount Carmel" (I Kings 18:20). The omission of any mention of Jezebel at this critical juncture is remarkable. We can only think of one gathering in the Holy Land more momentous in its results than that on Mount Carmel. All four Evangelists record a multitude gathered outside Pilate's palace in Jerusalem, led by the highest ecclesiastics of the nation. A great decision had to be made. Barabbas the robber, and the blessed Son of God, Israel's Messiah, were set before the people of their choice. "Not this man, but Barabbas," was their united cry. Yet that multitude

were not Baal worshippers as those with whom Elijah
had to do; they were the professed worshippers of
Jehovah, and they regarded with abhorrence the
idolatries of their fathers! Yet they would not have
Jehovah's Christ; a robber was more to their taste! Fatal
decision, from which the blinded nation is suffering to
this day? "His blood be on us, and on our children,"
said they (Matt. 27:25); and the God of righteousness
has held them to their word.

We borrow the words of another concerning the
meeting on Mount Carmel. "There are few more
sublime stories in history than this. On the one hand the
solitary servant of Jehovah, accompanied by his one
attendant; with his wild shaggy hair, his scanty garb,
and sheepskin cloak, but with (calm dignity of
demeanour) and the minutest regularity of procedure,
repairing the ruined altar of Jehovah with twelve stones,
– on the other hand the eight hundred and fifty
prophets of Baal and Ashtaroth, doubtless in all the
splendour of their vestments, with (the wild din of their
vain repetitions and the maddened fury of their
disappointed hopes, and the silent people surrounding
all" (Dr. W. Smith). It is not quite certain that the
prophets of Ashtaroth were present, possibly Jezebel
was able to protect her own protégées, although the
feeling amongst the people was too strong to allow her
to prohibit the gathering altogether. Elijah wished the
two hosts of misleaders to attend, but mention is only
made of Baal's four hundred and fifty (I Kings. 18:19,
22, 40).

Elijah addressed himself to the people direct. When
rulers transgress against God, and bring down His
chastening hand, it is always the poor who suffer most.
Probably Ahab and Jezebel had not been short of wine
and meat during the famine; and false prophets can

always be trusted to look well after themselves. So "Elijah came unto all the people, and said, How long halt ye between two opinions? If Jehovah be God, follow Him; but if Baal, then follow him" (I Kings 18:21. This day must be a day of decision, and the people doubtless felt the reasonableness of what Elijah said. The nation was at that time divided into three classes:— there were hordes of evil religious leaders; there were at least a few thousand who were still true in heart to Jehovah (although did not seem to be aware of their existence); and there was the mass of the people who were apparently indifferent to what form religion might take, but they wanted rain! These three classes are represented to-day in the nations of Christendom. There are religious misleaders, some of whom, pompously describe themselves as "Higher Critics," who would destroy all faith in God and His Word; and others, ritualistically inclined, would enslave the multitudes to the Italian clique in the Vatican. These two groups are largely responsible for the terrible disasters of our time. In contrast with these, God has in every land a pious remnant who loves His Word, although perhaps they are not as outspoken in testimony as they should be. There then are the masses, who care nothing for "religion". Christianity, Judaism, Mohammedanism, etc. are much alike to them; but they do not wish to be disturbed, and they cannot see why God should punish the nations for this condition of things. These people need to be brought to the point of decision. Is there a God; why not obey Him? Is there a Saviour; why not trust Him? To which of these three classes does the reader belong? Reader, is your mind made up that the God of Heaven is the only true God; that the Lord Jesus, His beloved Son, is the only possible Saviour; and that His precious blood can alone cleanse from sin, and give you a title to eternal bliss?)

Elijah spoke a second time to the people, again ignoring both king and prophets, and also any officials who may have been in attendance upon the king. His proposal was very simple: two bullocks were to be provided, one for Baal's four hundred and fifty prophets, and one for himself – Jehovah's solitary witness that day. (Where was Obadiah?). Each bullock was to be cut in pieces and laid on wood, with no fire under, and the prophets of Baal were to call upon the name of their god, and Elijah would call upon the name of Jehovah; and the God that answered by fire was to be Israel's God. The people, well knowing that Baal was the reputed god of fire, said, "It is well spoken." To Elijah's appeal, "How long halt ye between two opinions?" they answered not a word; but the proposal to submit the great question to a trial by fire was so reasonable that "all the people answered and said, it is well spoken."

Elijah then turned to the prophets of Baal, and said, "Choose you one bullock for yourself, and dress it first; for ye are many; and call on the name of your gods, but put no fire under" (I Kings 18:25). It was important to stress the last clause when dealing with unprincipled villains. Priestly "miracles" have a bad reputation for imposture. In the calmness of faith, Elijah could afford to allow the emissaries of Satan to move first, knowing quite well that the god they served had no power.

What a day it was! From morning until noon the prophers cried, "O Baal, answer us!" realizing that for them everything was at stake. The silence of their deity threw them into a frenzy, and they leaped about the altar they had made. "The idols of the nations are silver and gold, the work of men's hands. They have mouths, but they speak not; eyes have they, but they see not, they have ears, but they hear not; neither is there any breath in their mouths. They that make them are like unto them: so is every one that trusteth in them" (Ps. 135:15-18).

With the multitudes looking on, when noon came Elijah mocked the unhappy prophets. He suggested that they were not crying loudly enough; perhaps their god was occupied with other business, and could not attend to them; possibly he was away from home; or he might be asleep! Goaded by these taunts, the false prophets gashed themselves with swords and spears until their bodies streamed with blood! This unholy farce on the part of men made in the image of God was suffered to continue three hours longer.

At "the time of the offering of the evening sacrifice" Elijah judged that his opportunity had come. It was three p.m., and the evening lamb was being placed on the altar of Jehovah in Jerusalem, with its accompanying Meal offering and Drink offering, all speaking to God of Christ whose death at Calvary took place at that hour (Exod. 29:41; Matt. 27:46). It was the hour of divine blessing: compare Ezra 9:5; Dan. 9:21. The hour had struck for Elijah's sacrifice to be offered, and for the blessing which followed.

"Come near unto me," said Elijah to the people, so long led astray like foolish sheep. There is a sound of tenderness in the prophet's words, reminiscent of Joseph's invitation to his guilty and trembling brethren in Gen. 45:4. Elijah would soon now lead the poor misguided people back to their long-suffering and faithful God. In their presence he repaired the long-dishonoured altar of Jehovah. He would teach them the true way of approach to God. If blessing was ever again to be enjoyed in Israel, it must be in virtue of the divinely accepted sacrifice. When the remnant returned

from Babylon with Zerubbabel "they set the altar upon
his bases, for fear was upon them because of the people
of those countries: and they offered burnt offerings
thereon unto Jehovah, even burnt offerings morning
and evening" (Ezra 3:2-3). In their weakness they felt
the altar would be a better protection than walls and
weapons. They were right, for the altar and sacrifices
spoke to God of Christ, and God always responds to
faith of that character.

Elijah built his altar of twelve stones "according to
the number of the tribes of the sons of Jacob, unto
whom the word of Jehovah came, saying, Israel shall be
thy name." This act is proof of the prophet's spiritual
perception. The twelve tribes were no longer walking in
unity; their unity has not been restored to this day, nor
will it be until the kingdom of the Lord Jesus (Ezek.
37:21-23). Elijah was standing on ten-tribe ground; but
his twelve stones tell us that he entered into God's
thoughts about His people. The people were still one in
His mind. Although the temple in Jerusalem was now
only recognised by two tribes, the High Priest still bore
the names of all the children of Israel on his breast plate
before Jehovah, and twelve loaves were still placed on
the table of shewbread in the holy place (Exod. 25:30
Lev. 24:5-8). Two centuries after the great gathering on
Mount Carmel Hezekiah, King of Judah, at the
Passover that he held in Jerusalem commanded that
atonement should be made for *all* Israel (2 Chron.
29:24). Yet only two tribes acknowledged his sway, and
the deportation of the Northern tribes had already
begun! After the return from Babylon "the children of
those that has been carried away, which were come out
of the captivity, offered burnt offerings unto the God of
Israel, twelve bullocks for *all* Israel (Ezra. 8:35). Six
centuries later still, James addressed an epistle "to the

twelve tribes which are scattered abroad, greeting." All this was very precious to God, as showing that Elijah, Hezekiah, Ezra, and James entered into His thoughts concerning His faulty people. Are we as spiritually intelligent to-day? As we look around us, we see Christ's members, not in two parts as Israel in the days of the kings, but in divisions almost innumerable. Do we sorrow about this before our God, and do we seek to contemplate His saints (however faulty they may be) as He contemplates them? Do we refuse to sanction this unholy confusion? Are we able to say in faith "there is one body and one Spirit, even as we are called in one hope of our calling?" (Eph. 4:4).

Elijah having built his altar, made a trench around it; and when he had laid his burnt sacrifice upon it, he commanded to pour four barrels of water over it. He repeated this three times, until the bullock and the wood were drenched, and the trench became a moat! He would thus appear to put every possible difficulty in the way that the impending miracle might be the more convincing. The prophets of Baal did not venture to use water thus, but Elijah used it freely. He then drew near, and offered his simple prayer: "Jehovah, God of Abraham, Isaac, and of Israel, let it be known this day that Thou art God in Israel, and that I am Thy servant, and that I have done all things at Thy word. Hear me, O Jehovah, hear me, that the people may know that Thou art the Lord God (Jehovah Elohim), and that Thou hast turned their heart back again" (I Kings 18:36-37). It should be observed that the prophet sought no honour for himself (unlike Simon of Samaria who "gave out that himself was some great one" – Acts 8:9); he kept his true place as a mere servant, acting at the word of his God. Like Paul, he would have said, "I am nothing" (2 Cor. 12:11; 1 Cor 3:7). Do not miss the lesson, good reader!

Elijah proved the truth of Isa. 65:24: "it shall come to pass, that before they call, I will answer: and while they are speaking, I will hear." Israel must wait for this blessed experience until the glorious age when "the wolf and the lamb shall feed together." Elijah had it while facing a whole pack of wolves with teeth undrawn! It is good to have to do with God. His answer to the lonely man's prayer was prompt and decisive. "Then the fire of Jehovah fell, and consumed the burnt sacrifice, and the wood, and the stones, and the dust, and licked up the water that was in the trench."

Let not the reader miss a word of this remarkable verse. The fire – the emblem of the righteous judgement of God – might well have fallen upon the disobedient nation, or, passing by the nation, it might have fallen upon Ahab and his hundreds of idolatrous prophets – all servants of the Devil; but it did nothing of the kind. The fire fell upon the unoffending bullock which Elijah had placed upon the altar! What a picture of the great sacrifice of Calvary! There the righteous judgement of God fell, not upon the wicked masses of men, nor even upon the unprincipled leaders, who were primarily responsible for that cross being set up; the judgement of God in all its terrible severity fell upon the Holy One who hung there, so that He was constrained to cry, "My God, My God, why hast Thou forsaken Me?" (Matt. 27:46). That stupendous sacrifice, the full value of which is only known to God, has made blessing possible for sinners everywhere; and the first preachers of the Gospel were even commanded to begin at Jerusalem with their proclamation of repentance and remission of sins in the Saviour's name! (Luke 24:47). Faith sees Him now risen and glorified at God's right hand, clear proof that for Him, and for all who trust Him, the judgement of God is past for ever.) The effect of the fire from heaven at Carmel was marvellous. "When all the people saw it, they fell on their faces: and they said: "Jehovah, He is the God; Jehovah, He is the God." The great decision was made; and God, who is compassionate for nations as well as for individual sinners, could now grant blessing. The rain would soon descend!

But what about the prophets of Baal? They were not destroyed by the fire of God; there was thus, for a brief moment, a door open for repentance. Their exhausted and bleeding bodies were suffcient proof that Baal was worthless. He could do nothing for his most ardent votaries in their hour of peril. They stood publicly convicted of having practised fraud upon the people. Why did they not immediately fall upon their faces, and confess their great sin before God and the nation? They did nothing of the kind; sullen and defiant, they stood upon the mountain in the presence of the people they had cruelly deceived for many years: and even the king's partiality for them could not now save them from destruction. In obedience to Deut. 13:1-5 (which meant nothing to Ahab), Elijah commanded that all the prophets were to be arrested. Willing hands obeyed, and the whole ghastly host, four hundred and fifty in number, were led down to the brook Kishon, and slain. Have we learned to distinguish between the ways of God in different dispensations? From Moses until Christ was the age of law. Among other righteous enactments, death was the penalty for false teaching. It is otherwise in this day of grace. Those who would mislead souls concerning the fundamentals of the faith must be sternly rejected; even a widow and her children were admonished by John in his Second Epistle not to show such persons even the courtesies of life; but beyond this we have no authority to go. Rome has judged otherwise in her ignorance of divine grace, and blind disregard of the Word of God. Many a choice servant of Christ has been cruelly slaughtered under the pretence of getting rid of "dangerous heretics." When the servants in the parable of the tares in the wheatfield enquired if they should gather up the tares, the Lord replied: "Nay; lest while ye gather up the tares, ye root up also the wheat with them. Let both grow together until the harvest" etc. (Matt. 13:29-30). Perhaps no words from our Lord's lips have been more generally misunderstood than these. They have frequently been quoted as a plea for retaining unsound persons in Church fellowship. But the Church is not in view in the parable of the wheat and the tares; indeed the Church had never been spoken of up to that time. The parable is found in Matt. 13; but the Lord's first mention of the Church is in Chap. 16: "Grow together" does not mean "fellowship together"; impossible that He who is Holy and True should appear to sanction such confusion (Rev. 3:7). The wheat and the tares are to grow together in the field, and the Lord Himself has taught us that "the field is the world" (Matt. 13:38). In other words, those who are true to Christ, and love His truth must not put to death false teachers, even if they had power to do so. Such delicate work as weeding God's wheatfield could not be entrusted to fallible men; terrible miscarriages of justice would inevitably follow.

If any would inquire as to what is meant by the "destruction of the flesh" in I Cor. 5:5, it is not the body that is referred to, but the evil moral principle that is connected with the body in us all. "Delivering unto Satan," as in I Cor. 5:5 and I Tim. 1:20 is apostolic action; in the first case operating in conjunction with the assembly and in the second apart from the assembly altogether. The evil persons in question, having failed to learn their lessons in God's gracious school, had to be broken and humbled by Satan's cruel instrumentality. Divine discipline in all its forms is a deeply serious matter, but always with ultimate blessing in view, "that the spirit may be saved in the day of the Lord Jesus."

Our duty is to "put away" from amongst ourselves wicked persons. Further we must not go.

The Prophet and His God

THE people having given their decision, and the idolatrous prophets having been slain, Elijah knew that rain was near. Accordingly he said to Ahab: "Get thee up, eat and drink, for there is a sound of abundance of rain" (I Kings 18:41). Let us observe that the welcome rain did not begin to fall immediately the people shouted, "Jehovah, He is the God." In the divine ordering, Elijah must first pray for it. He was, so to speak, God's administrator towards Israel at that crisis. His lips pronounced the judgement; and his lips must announce the blessing; but both blessing and judgement were preceded by prayer. Thus we have the prophet going up to the top of Carmel to speak to God. Ahab, in his selfishness, prepared to go home; not to pray, but to feast. He had the feeling that the long continued drought was ending. That was all that mattered: there would soon be food again for his horses and mules! Meantime, a banquet was more to his liking than a prayer-meeting!

But where was Obadiah? The Lord has taught us in Matt. 18:19 the preciousness of two praying together;

but the two must be in harmony; they must both be alike in separation to God, and walking in His ways for their prayers to be effectual. Alas, there was no bond of sympathy between Elijah and Obadiah, although both were men born of the Spirit! Obadiah did not stand by Elijah when he confronted the foe, nor did he bow the knee with him when he made supplication to God. How much Obadiah missed by pandering to the world, accepting ease and honour in the midst of the ungodly! Also, how much Jonathan missed by not separating himself from the divinely rejected Saul – order of things to go outside with David! He could never have written David's psalms! "Ye are honourable," wrote the Apostle to the ease-loving Corinthians, "but we are despised" (I Cor. 4:10). But Paul was more happy than they, nevertheless. To stand apart from the world-system is admittedly loss, as men judge; but the spiritual gain in communication with God is immense.

Surely Elijah needed to eat and drink as well as Ahab! The events of the day were exhausting, and the servants of God get hungry and tired as well as other men. Even the Son of God sat in weariness on the well of Sychar while His disciples went into the town to buy food. But the spiritual rises about the physical. The immediate needs of the body are forgotten when powerful spiritual interests are operating. When the disciples returned, and begged the Lord to eat, He replied, "I have meat to eat that ye know not of." His spirit had been deeply refreshed by His conversation with the Samaritan woman (John 4). In like manner Elijah rose above his bodily needs, and gave himself to prayer.

The knowledge that God means to give does not make prayer unnecessary. Thus in Ezek. 36-37 Jehovah, after having declared in a very full way His purposes of grace concerning Israel, said, "I will yet for this be inquired of by the house of Israel to do it for them." Elijah bowed himself upon the earth, and put his face between his knees. A becoming attitude, surely! He who stood bold and erect before king, prophets, and people now takes the lowest possible place before God. His success had not elated him. His name would become famous when the report of Carmel got abroad throughout Israel, Judah, and other lands, but the prophet was not seeking glory for himself. He was just Jehovah's servant, and had acted according to His Word. Having fulfilled his commission, he got down low at the feet of Him who sent him.

Brethren, prayer is no light matter. It is a wonderful thing to enter into the presence of the Divine Majesty! His greatness and our littleness should be remembered; but oh the privilege in this day of being able to draw near to the Father in the name of the Son, in the power of the Holy Spirit!

The prophet who, three and a half years previously, prayed "Withhold the rain," now prays "Send the rain." But even so (and doubtless Elijah had intercourse with Jehovah about the matter before the great gathering took place) the answer to his prayer was not immediate. He said to his servant (was it the widow's son whom he had raised from the dead?): "Go up now, look toward the sea." He returned saying, "There is nothing." It frequently pleases God to test the faith of His people; but He encourages us to "continue in prayer, and watch in the same with thanksgiving" (Col. 4:2); also to "pray always with all prayer and supplication in the Spirit" (Eph. 6:18). The widow of Luke 18: 2-5 was probably not a mere parabolic character, but an actual person whom the Lord has observed. Her perseverance attracted Him. She had a grievance, and she took it to the judge; but he was not disposed to burden himself with the matter. But the woman persevered. Morning after morning when the doors of the Court were opened, in walked that widow! Let no reader misunderstand the application. God is not indifferent, and unwilling to bless; and certainly He would not despise a suppliant because she was poor and a widow; it is the woman's *perseverance* that He bids us remember and emulate. One wonders what would happen if some person accosted us when coming away from a prayer-meeting, and were to ask what we have prayed for? Could we always give a coherent answer? The widow could have given a very plain reason why she attended the Court.

Elijah said to his servant, "Go again seven times". Seven is God's number of perfection. The seventh time the young man said, "Behold, there ariseth a little cloud out of the sea, like a man's hand." The Lord Jesus said to the people in His day, "When ye see a cloud rise out of the West (and Elijah's servant was looking towards the West) straightway ye say, there cometh a shower; and so it is" (Luke 12:54). The "man's hand" is suggestive. Belshazzar saw the fingers of a man's hand writing upon the plaster of the wall of his palace, and it pronounced his doom (Dan. 5:5). There is a Man into whose hand God has committed both judgement and blessing for men; judgement bye-and-bye, blessing now (Acts 17:31). Israel having become repentant, and having judged the evil that was amongst them, blessing was now to be granted.

The little cloud was enough for Elijah. He sent a message to Ahab, who apparently had not yet left the mountain: "Prepare thy chariot, and get thee down, that the rain stop thee not." The longed-for rain fell heavily. "It came to pass in the meanwhile, that the heavens were black with clouds and wind, and there was a great rain." Elijah was so overjoyed he did a remarkable thing. "The hand of Jehovah was on Elijah; and he girded up his loins, and ran before Ahab to the entrance of Jezreel" (1 Kings 18:46). He must have been both tired and hungry, and he was probably a man advanced in years; yet he made himself the king's footman in the joy of his heart. Things seemed to be getting right again amongst the people of God; and that was everything to the man who loved Jehovah and His people. In like spirit David danced before Jehovah with all his might when the ark of the covenant was carried up into Zion (2 Sam. 6:14). Neither prophet nor king thought of dignity on those great occasions! The Lord has told us there is joy in the presence of God over one sinner that repenteth; and John writing to his friend Gaius says, "I have no greater joy than to hear that my children walk in the truth" (3 John 4). These are pure joys of which this unhappy world, in its estrangement from God knows nothing; but unless we, God's saints, are walking in communion with Him, such joys will not appeal to our hearts as they should.

Flight

WE may perhaps wonder that Elijah, a man so morally superior to Ahab, should run before his chariot from Carmel to Jezreel – no mean journey. He would "honour the king," as we are exhorted to do in I Pet. 3:17. This is always the becoming attitude of God's saints towards the supreme ruler, irrespective of what his personal character may be. The ruler, whoever he may be, at any time, or in any land, is God's representative. He may be too ungodly to understand this himself; but faith understands it, and acts accordingly.

We picture the prophet arriving in the city drenched with rain, very hungry and very tired; but should he have gone there at all? He doubtless meant well, even as Paul in his last journey to Jerusalem (Acts 21). The express word of Jehovah took Elijah to Cherith, to Zarephath, and twice into Ahab's presence; but the word of Jehovah is not mentioned in connection with his run to Jezreel. Had he forgotten Jezebel? That violent woman was a force to be reckoned with, but not at all to be feared by a man of faith conscious that God was directing his steps. The Lord taught His disciples to pray, "lead us not into temptation" (Matt. 6:13); for we do not realize how weak we are until we are tested. If it be urged that "the hand of Jehovah was on Elijah," thus giving him strength for the journey, that does not prove that Jehovah was sending him. For an angel was sent from heaven to provide a meal for him when he was fleeing to Horeb, a journey which was most certainly not undertaken by the word of Jehovah.

Poor weak Ahab, on his return from Carmel, told Jezebel all that had taken place there, and particularly the destruction of the prophets. In her fury, Jezebel sent a message to Elijah: "So let the gods do to me, and more also, if I make not thy life as the life of one of them by tomorrow about this time" (I Kings 19:2). This appears to have followed quickly, and thus the messengers would find, the prophet at a low ebb physically. He seemed unable to view the threat calmly, or even to spread it out before Jehovah. A little reflection would have suggested to him that the threat was a practically empty one; for why should Jezebel give him a day's notice of her intention to kill him? Her messenger could easily have slain him at once, as

Herod's executioner beheaded John the Baptist (Mark 6:27). It rather looks as if Jezebel's real aim was to drive Elijah out of the country, lest his influence became too strong to suit her evil purposes. Public opinion was in favour of the prophet at this juncture, and it might not be polite to murder him! It is said of Chrysostom of Constantinople that when the Empress Eudoxia sent him a threatening message, he replied, "Go, tell her Majesty that I fear nothing but sin." But nothing of this seemed possible for Elijah at this critical moment. It has been truly said that faith in us is never more feeble than immediately after a great victory. We see this in David. He gained a moral triumph over himself in I Sam. 26, when he had Saul in his power, and refused to hurt him; the next thing we read is: "David said in his heart, I shall perish one day by the hand of Saul: there is nothing better for me than that I should speedily escape into the land of the Philistines" (I Sam. 27:1). What a collapse of faith! God had carried David safely through many perils; now confidence seemed at an end! So with Elijah in I Kings 19. With calm courage he had confronted multitudes on Mount Carmel; now he is terror-stricken by the voice of a woman! Peter was bold enough in the garden in the presence of soldiers; but became an abject coward when amongst the servant-maids! Real danger he faced boldly; where no danger appears to have been, he feared the worst! What poor creatures we are! King, prophet, and apostles thus broke down! Are we better than they? Let us watch and pray, lest we enter into temptation (Matt. 26:41). Certain Pharisees approached the Lord Jesus one day, saying: "Get Thee out, and depart hence: for Herod will kill Thee." God's perfect Servant saw through the move. Herod himself had inspired that message. He wished to get rid of Jesus out of his borders; but he had no wish to repeat the crime of murder, for the death of John the Baptist still troubled his conscience. But the Lord refused to be deflected from the path of duty (Luke 13:31-33). When the last evening arrived, He went, as He was wont, to the mount of Olives, well knowing what awaited Him there (Luke 22:39).

Jezebel's threat overwhelmed Elijah. "When he saw that, he went for his life". Unlike Paul, who said: "None of these things move me, neither count I my life dear unto myself" (Acts 20:24). "I am ready to die at Jerusalem for the name of the Lord Jesus" (Acts 21:13).

"When he saw *that*!" Everything depends upon what our eyes see whether we are strong or weak. The sight of the glorified Christ strengthened Stephen to suffer and die; and Paul to suffer and live (Col. 1:2). Elijah was no longer able to say, "As Jehovah the God of Israel liveth, before whom I stand." For the time being, his eyes were not upon God. His departure from Jezreel was no mere retirement, as when our Lord went into the country in John 11:54; (it was *panic!*) It did not even occur to him to seek shelter in the dominions of pious King Jehoshaphat. He rushed through the kingdom to Beersheba in the far south. There he left his servant, and went still further, right outside God's land altogether!

Let us not miss the lesson of this. It is always possible for a man's personal faith to be unequal to the greatness of his testimony. In that case, the pressure of painful circumstances will cause a break-down sooner or later. Do we really mean all that we say? Is God indeed to our souls all that our praching would suggest? These are serious questions, which every witness for God should face. We must watch and pray lest circumstances arise which would reveal that we are not the men of faith we seem to be.

Elijah having gone a day's journey into the wilderness sat down under a juniper tree and spoke to God – probably his first word of prayer since he left Jezreel. "He requested for himself that he might die." Unbelief is always unreasonable and inconsistent. If the prophet really wished to die, why did he flee from Jezebel? Why not die a martyr's death in the midst of the people of God? Jehovah was no longer uppermost in his thoughts. The divine glory was not before his mind, but some fancied advantage for himself. (Life was now a disappointment! His work in Israel had gone all wrong!) *Self-Pity* How gracious of our God not to take His poor perverse servants always at their word! It was His intention that Elijah should not die at all; that he should have an exit from the world such as no-one ever had before, or has had since! Paul in Phil. I took a totally different line from Elijah. His work also had gone wrong (as men would judge), and he was in prison, with martyrdom threatening. Calmly in the presence of God he considered the situation. He was in a great "strait." If he put his own interest first, he would desire to depart and be with Christ, which would be happier for him than the happiest experiences here. But he thought of the need of the saints; therefore he desired to remain on earth a little longer; but in any case his one ambition was that Christ should be magnified in his body, whether by life or by death.

Elijah's prayer was brief and pointed as his manner was. "It is enough; now, O Jehovah, take away my life; for I am not better than my fathers." In the concluding words perhaps is contained the secret of his failure. Who ever said that he was better than his fathers? Possibly his success on Mount Carmel had inflated him. All alone he had accomplished great things for God. Did this really make him feel somewhat important and even indispensible? This is a condition of mind which can easily develop in any of us; but it is fatal to our usefulness. Many years ago, the writer called to say farewell to an aged servant of Christ just passing into the presence of his Lord. As we clasped hands at parting, he said: "Good-bye, beloved brother; remember, few men are important, and none are necessary." Wholesome words, not to be lightly forgotten! It is an unspeakable honour for the great God to make use of any of us in His work; but let us never imagine that He cannot do without us.

Elijah fell asleep. Well he might, for surely he was badly over-wrought. After some time (not too soon, we may be sure) an angel touched him, saying, "Arise and eat." Looking around, he saw a cake baken on hot stones, and a cruse of water; having refreshed himself, he slept again. Here we have a truly wonderful manifestation of the kindness of God. An angel sent from heaven to provide a meal for a faulty servant who had forsaken an important post of duty, and who was now completely outside the path of God's leading!

"To those who fall, how kind Thou art!
How good to those who seek!"

When we compare this angelic ministration with the prophet's experience at Cherith the conclusion is this: – when he was right with God, it was simply the need of his stomach which had to be considered, and the ravens sufficed for that service; but when he was all wrong with God, something more serious than his stomach was in question; God would reach his heart. The attentions of the angel would be a definite assurance to Elijah that Jehovah loved and cared for him still, spite of his deep failure. Elijah should have learned from this, God's feelings towards His erring people Israel. The prophet's complaints at Horeb will tell us that he did not feel towards the people as God did. A second time the angel awoke him, saying, "Arise and eat; because the journey is too great for thee." A journey that he should never have undertaken!

John 21 furnishes us with another instance of a meal provided by divine love for disobedient servants. It was not an angel, but the Lord Jesus Himself, who prepared that fish breakfast. Cold, wet, and hungry, the seven disciples who went fishing in self-will instead of waiting patiently for their expected Lord, were warmed and fed with no word of censure from His holy lips!

It is a precious thought that God never gives up His saints, however faulty they may be. At a Bible Reading long ago where it was being taught that the believer in Jesus stands in the eternal sunshine of God's favour, the question was asked, "But what if I turn my back upon Him?" The reply was given, "He will shine on your back!" God knew that His poor servant Elijah was physically over-wrought, and He handled him in suitability to his condition. Our contemptible foe delights to attack the children of God at such times, and too often he gains an advantage. The Lord Jesus had been forty days without food when Satan approached Him in the wilderness, and suggested to Him to make stones into bread, but he had no success with God's Holy One. Whether full or hungry, He refused to act in the smallest matters without a word from God (Matt. 4:4).

These pages are being written during times of greater stress than men have known since the world's foundation. Many beloved children of God are over-wrought. Frequent alarms; destruction of property; loss of loved ones; combined with lack of help in the duties of daily life, are telling their tale. With lowered physical vitality, the temptations of the Devil are serious; faith

E

can only be maintained at its true level by moment by moment dependence upon God. No circumstances are too serious for His abounding grace.

At the Mount of God

STRENGTHENED by the food so wonderfully provided, Elijah proceeded further into the wilderness. John the Baptist chose the wilderness for its possibilities of quiet communion with God (Luke 1:80); there is no evidence that Elijah went there with anything so commendable in his mind. For the time being, he had practically forgotten God! Terrible possibility for any of us in times of discouragement! After forty days the prophet reached Horeb, the mount of God – a place of peculiar interest. There Jehovah had dealings with Moses, forty years after his premature attempt to deliver His people. At Horeb Moses learned precious lessons which fitted him for his future service in Israel (Exod. 3). In the same neighbourhood was Mount Sinai, where Jehovah had dealings with the nation, and set before them His holy law (Exod. 20). It is significant that Elijah in his indignation against the people should have gone there. It was as if he desired judgment upon them for their unfaithfulness. The Holy Spirit in Rom. 2:2 says "he pleaded with God *against* Israel."

The prophet took shelter in a cave, and soon he heard the voice of Jehovah. He had heard the kindly words of the angel, but he had been out of touch with Jehovah for some time. The divine voice was a challenge: "What doest thou here, Elijah?" This reminds us of the Creator's call to disobedient Adam in the garden,

"Where art thou?" (Gen. 3:9), and also of His challenge to Cain, "What hast thou done?" (Gen. 4:10). Elijah heard no divine challenge either at Cherith or at Zarephath; for he went to both places by the word of Jehovah. But his presence at Horeb was a different matter. Jehovah did not send him there; but, being there he was taught lessons of the deepest possible importance, and the record of them has been preserved for our instruction to-day.

We note the word *"doest."* "What doest thou here?" Great stirrings were taking place in the land of Israel; for the mighty events on Mount Carmel must have made a deep impression upon the minds of the people. Jehovah was now the confessed God of Israel, and no longer Baal. How useful Elijah might have been as a worker and instructor amongst the masses at such a time; and there was indeed no-one else who could have done the work. But here is Elijah far away from the habitations of men, and sheltering in the quietness of a cave! When the Lord says to His servants, "Come ye apart and rest awhile," it is the right thing to cease labour and retire (Mark 6:31); but no such words had been addressed to Elijah. He was an absentee from an important post of duty at one of the most critical moments in his nation's history. Philip left Samaria when the tide of blessing was in full flow, and went down to a desert road; but the angel of the Lord directed him there, and he went unhesitatingly, although he probably wondered why (Acts 8:26).

Brethren, let us seek to be subject at all times to the controlling hand of God. Let us never move without His guidance and when we get it, let us go forward, like Paul and his friends in Acts 16:9-10, when they crossed the sea from Troas into Macedonia. One of the vital principles of Christianity is the presence on earth of the

Holy Spirit in testimony to the absent Christ. He employs as instruments whomsoever He will, and He is the true Director of all the operations. If we go where we should not, either for service or for pleasure, we may hear the divine challenge, "What doest thou here?" and what can we say in reply?

Elijah's reply was deplorable. "I have been very jealous for Jehovah the God of hosts: for the children of Israel have forsaken Thy covenant, thrown down Thine altars, and slain Thy prophets with the sword: and I, even I only, am left; and they seek my life, to take it away." Thus the disgruntled prophet spoke well of himself, and ill of God's people, and virtually called upon God to judge them. He had got a long way from God in his soul in expressing himself thus. The contrast with Moses after the people's worship of the golden calf is startling. When Jehovah proposed to wipe out the stiff-necked people, and make a fresh start with Moses, Moses would not hear of it. He pleaded the honour of Jehovah's great name; he entreated Him to remember Abraham, Isaac, and Israel; and even prayed God to blot him out of the book of life, if thereby the people might be forgiven! (Ex. 32). It was music to Jehovah to hear His servant pleading thus in the spirit of self-sacrifice for His erring people. What an anticipation of Christ! Moses never shone more brightly than on that day ot matchless intercession. Would that we could catch the spirit of it!

God spoke again to Elijah. "Go forth, and stand upon the mount before Jehovah." (Great manifestations of divine power followed.) "Jehovah passed by, and a great strong wind rent the mountains, and brake in pieces the rocks before Jehovah; but Jehovah was not in the wind; and after the wind an earthquake; but Jehovah was not in the earthquake; and after the earthquake a fire; but

Jehovah was not in the fire; and after the fire a still small voice" (1 Kings 19:11-12). Manifestations of power are from God, but they must not be confounded with God himself. Elijah had witnessed His power at Carmel; but because he no longer beheld such displays, it seemed difficult for him to realize that God was working at all. But he presently learned that a quiet gracious work was proceeding in many hearts in Israel of which he was unaware. God had use for the whirlwind for out of it He spoke in majesty to Job and his friends (Job 38:1; 40:6), and Nahum tells us "Jehovah hath His way in the whirlwind and in the storm." He has use "for the earthquake": what blessed results followed the shaking at the midnight hour in Philippi (Acts 16). An earthquake was one of God's witnesses to His Son at the moment of His death (Matt. 27:51). He has also use for the fire, as the people of Israel had so recently proved on Mount Carmel. But although Elijah witnessed at Horeb the great and strong wind, the earthquake, and the fire, it was the still small voice which made him feel that he was having to do with God.

It is possible for us to-day to get discouraged if the work of God in our hands does not move in striking ways. Persons of energetic disposition, such as Elijah certainly was, are more likely than others to feel thus. Where there are no visible manifestations we are apt to conclude that nothing is doing at all! The Book of the Acts is instructive in this connection. God used the violence of an earthquake to arouse the Philippian jailor; He opened the very heavens to reach and lay low Saul of Tarsus; but Timotheus and Lydia were reached by the quiet influence of the Word of God with nothing notable connected with their conversion. A prominent London business man in the last century, who was a

F

lover of the Gospel (as we all should be) threw himself very zealously into the great inter-denominational campaigns of his day; but in the evening of life he said to me: "If I had my time over again, I would let all such movements alone. Enormous expenses were incurred, and I do not feel sure of the results. Upon mature reflection, I think perhaps the best work is done in the constant plodding in modest halls." I replied: "I told you that years ago." Those who want great things, and who are filled with Elijah's zeal and energy, would do well to remember what the London merchant said. Too often the great things involve the use of worldly methods, and also the sacrifice of divine principles which we profess to hold dear. These remarks are not intended to discourage enterprise for God. Far from it. If there are no signs of blessing in connection with the work we are doing, let us get down before God about it, and ask Him why our labour appears to be in vain. But the comparatively few souls that we can show as the result of quiet Scriptural preaching may be worth more in the long run than the crowds who are registered as converts because they have signed "decision cards," or have shaken hands with the preacher! Some of these souls may possibly be injured for life by such flippant handling.

There were no great things to show in Jerusalem after the return from the captivity; but real solid work was wrought which delighted the heart of God. By the hand of Zechariah the prophet Jehovah sent this encouraging message to the leader of the people. "This is the word of Jehovah to Zerubbabel: not by might, nor by power, but by My Spirit, saith Jehovah of hosts " (Zech. 4:6). Again we say it was the still small voice which made Elijah feel that he was having to do with God. It is the same to day. God speaks now to consciences and hearts in the written Word. The band, the choir, the solo, and other forms of religious excitement are unlikely to lay bare the conscience, and create in the hearer a horror of sin and its eternal consequences; such unapostolic methods would rather tend to hinder the voice of God reaching the inner man at all.

Jehovah's manner of approach to His fugitive servant was very gracious. He did not address him angrily in tones of thunder. The "soft gentle voice" (J.N.D.) did not terrify Elijah. It drew him to the mouth of the cave with his face reverently wrapt in his mantle. Servant and Master were now, as it were, face to face. A second time He who alone should control the movements of His servants put the question, "What doest thou here, Elijah?" The poor prophet repeated word for word what he said when first challengd. The children of Israel were so evil, they had forsaken Jehovah's covenant, thrown down His altars, and slain His prophets. Elijah alone remained; and he also they sought to kill! Such words were very grievous to Him who loved His people with everlasting love (Jer. 31:3). Since Elijah's day they have murdered the Son of God; even so, we are told in Rom. 11:28 they are still "beloved for the fathers' sake." Let us tread softly when we examine the failures of the servants of God. Elijah at Horeb, and Paul in Jerusalem (Acts 21) were out of the path of divine leading. The story of their faults is written for our warning. We do not feel worthy to stand alongside such devoted servants of God, but we must face the fact that they were not perfect. The Lord Jesus could have said all that Elijah said concerning rebellious Israel, and more! Was He not tasting the bitterness of malignant rejection? Yet not a word of complaint passed His lips, not a word that pleaded for judgment upon His enemies. Instead, He wept over them; and even when on the way to Calvary,

He said: "Father, forgive them; for they know not what they do" (Luke 23:34). Centuries before His coming the Spirit of prophecy put these words into His lips: "I have laboured in vain; I have spent My strength for nought, and in vain" (Isa. 49:4). But His labour was acceptable to the One who sent Him, and there His heart rested. Although treated by the people of Israel worse than Elijah, He did not flee away. We have seen already that when a hint was sent to Him to depart hence, or Herod would kill Him, He refused to do so, because His work was not finished. At the same moment He spoke of the people (of Jerusalem particularly) as having killed the prophets, but He said it in grief, not in anger (Luke 13:31-35). Psa. 16:8 explains the difference between the Lord Jesus and Elijah: "I have set Jehovah always before Me; because He is at My right hand, I shall not be moved." "Always" was not true of our prophet. When Jehovah was indeed before him, he was bold as a lion; but when he lost sight of Jehovah, and got Jezebel before him, be collapsed utterly. Truly, God has only had one perfect Servant. Let follow Him!

Jehovah's reply to Elijah's complaint is deeply solemn in all its parts. "Go return!" Every false step with any of us must be retraced. Abram should not have gone down into Egypt, and he enjoyed no more communion with God until he returned "unto the place of the altar, which he had made there at the first; and there Abram called on the name of Jehovah" (Gen. 13:4). But false steps and careless walking involve loss of time; so we are taught in the law of the Nazarite (Num. 6:12). Life is too short to allow of wasted time! Life on earth is our great preparation for ETERNITY!

To proceed with Jehovah's words to Elijah. "Go return on thy way to the wilderness of Damascus: and when thou comest, anoint Hazael to be king over Syria:

and Jehu the son of Nimshi shalt thou anoint to be king over Israel: and Elisha the son of Shaphat of Abel-Meholah shalt thou anoint to be prophet in thy room. And it shall come to pass, that him that escapeth the sword of Hazael shall Jehu slay: and him that escapeth from the sword of Jehu shall Elisha slay. Yet I have left Me seven thousand in Israel, all the knees which have not bowed unto Baal, and every mouth which hath not kissed him." The judgments which Elijah seemed to feel were necessary should be executed. The forsaken covenant, the desecrated altars, and the murdered prophets, should all be avenged; the circumstances of the judgments should be analogous to the whirlwind, the earthquake, and the fire. A ruthless destroyer from without, and a fierce reformer within, should be let loose upon the guilty nation.

Elijah was now to go to Abel-Meholah (in Naphtali) to anoint Elisha to be prophet in his room. He probably did not expect anything quite as serious as all this when "he made intercession to God against Israel" (Rom. 11:2-5). The principal lesson that he learned at Horeb was that Jehovah had seven thousand in Israel that were still true to Him, and refused Baal. Elijah had seen the terrible evils which covered the land, but somehow he had over-looked the good that was there. Had he known that Jehovah still had thousands of true hearts in Ahab's dominions, he would scarcely have said: "I, even I only am left!" Self-occupation is a spiritually ruinous thing, whatever form it may take; but it is highly objectionable when it leads any servant of God to imagine that he is the last true man upon earth! The testimony of God has never yet depended upon the slender thread of a human life, and it never will. God Himself will take care of the testimony; and in His own infinite wisdom He always knows where to find instruments through whom He can speak to the consciences and hearts of the people. The prophet said nothing in response to the solemn words of Jehovah. What could he say?

God's Seven Thousand

ELIJAH left Horeb, and started on his long journey Northward with the words of Jehovah ringing in his ears (and we may hope, in his heart also): "I have left Me seven thousand in Israel, all the knees which have not bowed unto Baal, and every mouth which hath not kissed him." God has always had a loyal remnant, even in the darkest days of Israel and of Christendom. In Thyatira, where blasphemy and wickedness prevailed, there were those who had not "this doctrine," and had not known the depths of Satan (Rev. 2:24). To the angel of the Church in dead Sardis the Lord said: "Thou hast a few names which have not defiled their garments; and they shall walk with Me in white; for they are worthy" (Rev. 3:4). When the tide of evil is flowing strongly, some timid souls fear to declare themselves. Joseph of Arimathaea believed in Jesus, but secretly for fear of the Jews. Nicodemus was somewhat like him; but the appalling wickedness of the crucifixion gave these men courage, and brought them out into the light (John 19:38-42). Our Lord's chosen disciples who had professed loyalty to Him, one of them being particularly strong in his protestations, were all missing at the critical hour. One of the twelve –Matthew – records that when John the Baptist was murdered "his disciples came, and took up the body, and buried it" (Matt. 14:12). Surely Matthew's heart smote him as he penned those words! He and his fellow-disciples did not do for the Lord Jesus what the disciples of John did for their teacher. It is undisputably the will of God that those who revere His name and value His truth should stand forth boldly in testimony, whatever the danger may be; but if in their timidity any lack courage for this, God does not despise faith which reigns in their hearts.

Now here is an interesting thing: – no sooner had Jehovah told Elijah of the loyal seven thousand than He began to bring some of them out into prominence. Elijah, of course, knew of Obadiah, and of the prophets whom he had befriended; now Elijah was sent to seek out Elisha the son of Shaphat. Here then is one of the seven thousand. In the following chapter – I Kings 20 – we read of three more, although their names are not given (5:5 13, 28, 35). Then in Chap. 21 we find faithful Naboth; and in Chap. 22 we have Micaiah the son of Imlah, whom Ahab hated for his outspokenness and kept in prison. These are a few samples of the true-hearted minority living in the midst of apostate Israel.

It was a peaceful scene at Abel-Meholah. The rain for which Elijah had prayed had done its work, and the land was ready for ploughing. The man to whom he was sent was thus engaged. The fact that twelve yoke of oxen were in use indicates that Elisha's father was a farmer in a large way. Elisha thus turned his back on good prospects when he accepted the call to follow Elikah. This is what God loves to see in those who serve Him. There are many in our day who say they are "out in the work." This means that they no longer evangelize after office hurs, but now devote their whole time to the service. Certainly if their ambition is to go from door to door and from town to town in search for souls, it is well that they should be free from everything else. But, my brethren, what has the step cost you? have you surrendered something substantial (as men speak) in order to serve the interests of Christ in a needy world? Many years ago a brother in an English town wrote me confidentially for advice. He could not make his shop pay, and he wondered whether the Lord would have him close it, and go forth to preach. What did I think? I replied that the Lord has no use for ne'er-do-wells. A poor grocer would not be likely to make a good preacher. If his business were at the height of prosperity and he felt the urge of the Gospel, the Lord would be delighted with the sacrifice. A different case was that of a young Englishman who held a good post with fine prospects who had China upon his heart. Just as he was posting his letter of resignation, a notification came from his employers that he was to be promoted to higher work with a considerable increase of salary! He hesitated not, but posted his letter, and in due course sailed for China. What God wants is men who are ready to tread the path of His beloved Son who "sold all that He had."

Elisha had nothing to gain as far as this world is concerned by following Elijah. The prophet was a proscribed man, and his life in continual peril. The Lord Jesus warned those who would follow Him that it might involve the loss of everything. Foxes had holes and birds had nests, but the Son of man had nowhere to lay His head (Matt. 8:20). Men called Him Beelzebub; what could His followers expect to be called? (Matt. 10:25). He was going onward to a cross; were His disciples willing to carry one? (Mark 8:34). Paul rejoiced to be treated as the filth of the world, and as the off-scouring of all things for Christ's sake (I Cor. 4:13). Do we seek ease and honour in the scene of our Lord's rejection?

(It has been said that Elijah was now to be superseded by Elisha. This seems hardly correct. Jehovah still had use for him as subsequent chapters show.) But meantime He would teach His servant that the testimony was in no real peril, and (He granted him the honour of training the man who should continue it." In the days (or perhaps years) that followed, Elijah had the comfort of Godly companionship,) His sense of loneliness had been too much for him, and had bred unbecoming thoughts in his mind. It is written of Elisha that "he poured water on the hands of Elijah" (2 Kings 3:11). Simple imagery, telling us how the younger man refreshed the elder. Paul experienced something of this in the loving ministrations of his son Timothy (Phil, 2:19-22).

*   *   *

We must not leave the subject of God's seven thousand without marking its application to ourselves in these closing days of the Christian era. Some who will read these pages have taken a definite stand in separation from the growing evils of Christendom. Popery, religious infidelity ("Higher Criticism"), and other forms of disobedience to the Word of God are marching on; and these separated ones abhor them all. This is good. Beware lest you allow discouragement, or anything else, to weaken the stand you have taken. But also beware how you speak of your brethren who (unaccountably to your minds) remain where they are. God knows their hearts; you do not. They are His saints; dear to Him for Jesus' sake. They cost Him more than you will ever fully understand, and in His own time He will cause them to shine forth in all the divine perfections of His Beloved Son. Speak no ill of them; judge them not. Some of their works, wrought amidst difficulties, are doubtless precious in His sight. It was

so even in corrupt Thyatira (Rev. 2:19). It may be that
the inconsistences of some professionally separated ones
have stumbled them – a most serious consideration
which should cause the deepest heart-searching before
God.

Elijah blundered in speaking ill of God's people.
Terrible words;– "he maketh intercession to God *against*
Israel" (Rom. 11:2). God will never tolerate this in any
one. Love them; pray for them, and instruct them in
meekness as God may give opportunity (2 Tim. 2:25). A
censorious attitude, may lead some to say: "No doubt
but ye are the people, and wisdom shall die with you"
(Job 12:2). The spirit that is characteristic of
Philadelphia is delightful to God; let us cultivate it. But
a supposititious Philadelphia may easily degenerate into
a very real Laodicea!

Naboth's Vineyard

SOLOMON says in Eccles, 2:4: "I made me great
works; I builded houses; and I planted
vineyards." Ahab could have said the same; but
what blessing did he get out of it all? The humble
prophet Elijah, whom he persecuted, is in Heaven; but
Ahab, alas! is not there. His father Omri built Samaria,
and made it the capital of his kingdom, but he seems to
have preferred Jezreel as a place of residence. In I Kings
22:39 we read of "the ivory house which he built,"
which was probably in Jezreel. He cast eyes upon the
vineyard of a neighbour, Naboth by name, and
demanded it; offering to give him a better vineyard in
exchange, or money if he wished. Naboth brought

Jehovah's name into the matter. It was not Ahab's custom to think of Jehovah, still less to seek His guidance about his doings. Naboth said: "Jehovah forbid it me that I should give the inheritance of my fathers unto thee" (I Kings 21:3). Let us be quite clear what was involved in this reply. (Our God would not wish His servants to be disobliging and un-neighbourly, but it was not such sentiments as these that guided Naboth in his refusal of the King's demand.) The land of Israel was unique in the earth. (It was Jehovah's land) in a very special sense (had He not a house there?), so much so that in Jer. 12:14 Jehovah speaks of the nations round about as "My evil neighbours". (The land had been distributed amongst the tribes by His direction, and every individual Israelite was responsible to regard himself as a tenant under his God.) He was thus not at liberty to alienate his portion. If he became poor, he might sell it until the Jubilee. "The land shall not be sold for ever, for the land is Mine; for ye are strangers and sojourners with Me. And in all the land of your posession ye shall grant a redemption for the land" (Lev. 25:23-24). Moreover, we gather from Num. 36 that even such a temporary sale must take place within the limits of the tribe, so that Jehovah's original distribution might not be disturbed. Ahab had no fear of God before his eyes; the Word of God had no place in his heart; and the year of Jubilee meant nothing to him. Had Naboth yielded to the king, it is not at all likely that the property would ever be returned. Also, Ahab probably belonged to a different tribe. In Ezek. 46:18 it is enacted that the priince who will rule for God in the holy land during the Millennial era must not take of the people's inheritance by oppression, "that My people be not scattered every man from his possession."

Naboth was thus a man of faith. His father valued

what Jehovah had given him, and Naboth valued it also. He would die rather than surrender what really belonged to God. The Naboth spirit seems rare in our time. Divine principles which our fathers prized, and for which many suffered the loss of everything, are very lightly regarded by their children. The worthies of past years are even regarded as over-scrupulous. A little of the accommodation spirit of the Twentieth Century would have been to their advantage! To be spoken of as a "Puritan" is considered a great reproach to-day!

us?

In the early days of the Nineteenth Century holy men with hearts aflame to learn the will of God, recovered for us priceless treasures of truth which ecclesiasticism had long obscured. Once more God's saints (or at least a remnant of them) realized their union with Christ risen and glorified and became detached in heart from things here. The blessed hope of His coming for His heavenly saints was disentangled from the judgements of God. The Church re-appeared to their soul's vision in its true relationships. It is Christ's body, to be in intimate association with Him in His glories, but meantime it is a vessel for the manifestation of His perfections here amongst men. It is God's house, the temple of the Holy Spirit, in which He graciously dwells, and where He delights to work sovereignly for the blessing of the members of Christ. Dr. C. I. Scofield, in the introduction of his well-known Bible, refers with appreciation to the "intensity and breadth of interest in Bible study unprecedented in the history of the Christian Church." Thus our "fathers" have handed down to us a priceless heritage; but do we value it? Have we sought to develop it further? Do we pore over the sacred page individually? Is it to us more to be desired than gold, and sweeter than honey and the honeycomb? (Ps. 19:10). Also do we delight to read it collectively; or have we sunk so low that we need to be entertained? Conferences, Rallies, Lantern lectures, and Solos are poor substitutes for the quiet, reverent, conversational Bible Readings in which our "fathers" delighted, and from which they drew their strength. Have we, in contrast with Naboth, sold our inheritance for "a better vineyard", or for money? Brethren, where are we? Have we really gone forth to Christ "without the camp, bearing His reproach" (Heb. 8:13); or have we merely exchanged a "Church" for a "Hall?"

Ahab returned home sulky after his talk with Naboth, and refused to eat. When Jezebel learned the cause, she moved promptly. She wrote letters to the Town Council, using the king's name and the royal seal. Her orders were peculiarly diabolical. The elders and nobles were to proclaim a fast, set Naboth at the head of the gathering, and bring in two sons of Belial (i.e., sons of worthlessness) to charge him with having cursed God and the king. We understand this to mean that they were to imagine some divine displeasure against their city; at the fast the cause was to be inquired into, with Naboth presiding; he whom they thus professed to honour was to be denounced as the "Achan" of the place, and hurried off to execution (Josh. 7:25). The whole business seems too horrible for belief; yet such was the moral degradation of Israel that all this was done by the queen and elders in God's name! (Baal had for the time being gone into the shade). It will be remembered that two wicked men were hired by the religious chiefs of Jerusalem to falsely accuse the Lord Jesus, that they might have some appearance of justification for putting Him to death (Matt. 26:60).

Jezebel's action in the case of Naboth was a dark foreshadowing of what Christendom's Jezebel has frequently been guilty of. Time-serving rulers and governors have been all too willing to put to a cruel death choice saints of God at the bidding of the so-called "Church." But God will remember all that has been done in Israel and in Christendom in the coming day of recompense. (Innocent blood will yet be avenged (Rev. 18:24). "Thou hast seen it, for Thou beholdest mischief and spite, to requite it with Thy hand" (Ps. 10:14).)

Not only was Naboth murdered, but his sons with him (2 Kings 9:26). The wicked elders would make certain that no heirs should arise to challenge what they had done.

(When Ahab was told by Jezebel that Naboth was dead, he went to the vineyard to take possession of it.) (Jehovah acted swiftly. He bade Elijah go and confront him in the blood-stained plot.) The wicked king quailed before the messenger of God. "Ahab said to Elijah, Hast thou found me, O mine enemy? And he answered, I have found thee; because thou hast sold thyself to work evil in the sight of Jehovah" (I Kings 21:20). (Ahab then had to listen to as fearful a sentence as was ever passed upon a sinner.) It was in three parts. (I) ("Behold, I will bring evil upon *thee*." He personally must suffer.) He came to a miserable end, as we know. (2) (His whole family was to be destroyed,) like the families of his evil predecessors Jeroboam and Baasha. (He had wiped out Naboth's family; God would wipe out his.) (3) (Jezebel was to be eaten by dogs.) (The fearful sentence concluded thus; "Him that dieth of Ahab in the city the dogs shall eat; and him that dieth in the field shall the fowls of the air eat.') (Hardened sinner though he was, Ahab was over-whelmed as he listened,) and he rent his clothes, put sackcloth upon his flesh, and went softly. (He knew that there was power in the words of God as uttered by Elijah. The God of all grace responded to Ahab's humiliation, and the greater part

of the sentence was postponed in its execution.))
Jehovah said to Elijah: "Seest thou how Ahab
hunbleth himself before Me? Because he humbleth
himself before Me, I will not bring the evil in his days:
but in his son's days will I bring evil upon his house."
God took into account the evil influence under which
he lived – "whom Jezebel his wife stirred up." But he
should never have married the woman, and he must
be held accountable for her iniquities (ver. 19); for the
man is the divinely appointed head of the woman,
whatever kind of woman she may be (I Cor. 11:3). Let
none of us overlook this!

Ahaziah and His Captains

MEN should learn lessons from the past, but do
they? Particularly where God's dealings are
involved men should profit; but the mind of
man is very obtuse in all things relating to God.
Belshazzar was quite aware of how Jehovah had
humbled Nebuchadnezzar; he knew also how Jehovah
took up the challenge when the proud king presumed to
cast three of His servants into the burning fiery furnace.
Yet he openly defied the God of Israel! Ahaziah knew
quite well when he began his reign of the great drought
which an indignant God had inflicted upon the nation
because of its idolatry. He knew also of the solemn
event on Mount Carmel, when Baal's prophets were
publicly confounded, and then slain; yet his short reign
of two years was marked by defiance of Jehovah! 1
Kings 22:52 records that "he did evil in the sight of
Jehovah, and walked in the way of his father, and in the

way of his mother" (for Jezebel still lived, and was still influential in the land). He copied Jeroboam's sins, and "served Baal, and worshipped him." Various events which followed one another quickly should have spoken to his conscience:– first, the tragic death of his father; second, the revolt of Moab after 150 years subjection to Israel; and third, his own accident. Wisdom would have taught him to enquire of God "is there not a cause?"

Finding himself a sick man through his fall out of a window, Ahaziah sent messengers to enquire of Baal-zebub, the god of Ekron whether he should recover (2 Kings 1). This was flagrant, for the recognition of Baal had been discouraged in the land, and Jehovah was (at least nominally) Israel's God. When Ahab's false prophets encouraged him to go to war with the Syrians, it was not Baal's name that they used, but the name of Jehovah (1 Kings 22:6). Baal-zebub means "lord of flies." The belief that flies carried disease led blind heathen to turn to this particular god for help; but Ahaziah should have known better. To enquire at Ekron was really to enquire of demons. Idols are nothing in themselves, but there are demons behind them, as 1 Cor. 10 teaches us. Traffic with demons is painfully common in our day. Men call it Spiritualism; "demonism" would be a more correct name for this great sin. This is unpardonable where Bibles abound, and where the Gospel of Christ is freely proclaimed. The moral and spiritual consequences of this unholy traffic are very serious.

An angel of Jehovah bade Elijah meet the messengers of the "King of Samaria" (he disdained to call such a man "King of Israel"), and ask them whether there was no longer a God in Israel that they must needs go to Ekron. They were to go back to their master, and tell him he would not recover, but would surely die. The messengers apparently awestruck, but without knowing that it was Elijah who had spoken to them went back to the king with the message. When Ahaziah enquired what kind of man it was who had thus intercepted them, they said it was "a man in a hairy garment, with a girdle of leather about his loins." The King at once recognised his father's dread monitor, he said, "It is Elijah the Tishbite!"

Not ashamed of his impiety, and in no wise humbled, Ahaziah ordered the arrest of the prophet. But why send a captain with fifty men (presumably armed) against a helpless old man? Conscience told the king that there was a mysterious power connected with Elijah which must be reckoned with. But what could soldiers do against the power of God? The captain found Elijah sitting on top of a hill. He said to him: "Thou man of God, the king hath said, come down." The prophet replied: "If I be a man of God, let fire come down from heaven and consume thee and thy fifty." The terrible thing took place forthwith. Such a disaster should have warned both the king and his officers that "it is a fearful thing to fall into the hands of the living God" (Heb. 10:31). But a second company was sent, as numerous as the first. The second captain was irritable. "O man of God, the king hath said, come down *quickly*." Military discipline is doubtless important. Officers and men, generally speaking, must obey their superiors; but every man, in every land, whether soldier or civilian, is, first of all, a servant of God, and he should on no account surrender his conscience. It will be no answer in the day of judgment that the king or government commanded this or that. "We ought to obey God rather than man" (Acts 5:29). The fact that both captains addressed Elijah as "man of God" proves that they had some idea that they were contending with God. It was no secret to any in Israel that at Elijah's word rain was withheld and fire descended; in other words, this humble man wielded the judgments of God. It was one thing to reject his testimony; it was quite another to attempt to destroy the man himself. God's name having been brought into the matter, He must needs take up the challenge. Ahaziah's father once benefited by the folly of the Syrians in this respect. The Syrians having said that Israel's God was God of the hills but not of the valleys, Jehovah asserted Himself, and granted Ahab a great victory, wicked man though he was (1 Kings 20:28). Thus, in the controversy between Ahaziah and Elijah, Jehovah again asserted Himself, and made the king and his people feel the might of His hand. The second captain was less excusable than the first. Knowing of the destruction of his predecessor, he impiously attempted the same thing, with the same fatal result.

What a contrast between Mount Carmel and the unnamed hill! At the one the fire of God consumed the sacrifice, but spared the people; at the other there was no sacrifice and the fire consumed the ungodly. The sacrifice of the Lord Jesus is a safe shelter for sinners; apart from that sacrifice, nothing but judgment is possible for any of us. Our Lord's disciples once referred to the destruction of Ahaziah's men. They were in the neighbourhood of that disaster; and they were indignant because the Samaritan people refused a welcome to the Lord. He was on his way to Jerusalem – a city of which they were jealous,, "Lord, wilt Thou that we command fire to come down from heaven; and consume them as Elias did?" (Luke 9:51-56). The Lord rebuked their mistaken zeal. God had not at that time sent Him to judge the world, but that the world through Him might be saved (John 3:17). At His second coming, "He shall smite the earth with the rod of His mouth, and with the breath of His lips shall He slay the wicked" (Isa. 11:4).

The poor human heart is slow to understand grace. Both Peter and Paul possessed miraculous powers – they could even raise the dead – but never once did either call down judgment upon his persecutors. With meekness they accepted all that came upon them for Jesus' sake, assured that in the wisdom of God everything would turn out to the furtherance of the Gospel. The cross of Jesus explains this. That blessed One could easily have smitten His foes; the fact that His captors fell to the ground at the sound of His voice was a warning to them as to this (John 18:6). When Peter became violent in the garden, He told him that a word of prayer to the Father would bring twelve legions of angels to His aid. But such a prayer He would not offer (Matt. 26:53).

The cross of Jesus was a necessity in the ways of God. Only on the ground of that great sacrifice could He give effect to His eternal counsels of grace. Righteousness having had its way, grace flows freely, yea, "the exeeding riches of His grace" (Eph. 2:7). The cross will yet be divinely avenged; but until the solemn day when God will change His attitude towards men, those who serve Him must be content to suffer. We cannot too frequently remind ourselves that we are followers of a rejected Christ. When He gets His vindication, we shall get ours also.

A third captain was sent against Elijah. He – wise man – fell upon his knees, and pleaded for his life and for the lives of his men. He realized that it was vain to contend with God. In David's day three companies of men were sent by Saul to take him and all three were equally willing for their evil work. But God had His own way of turning their efforts to folly (1 Sam. 19:21).

Ahaziah's third captain took very humble ground with the man of God. "I pray thee, let my life, and the lives of these fifty thy servants, be precious in thy sight." (2 Kings 1:13). Submission to God, represented by Elijah, saved those fifty one men. "Thy servants"; note the words addressed by a military officer to a humble Gileadite peasant. In like manner, no sinner need perish if he will but humble himself under the mighty hand of God (1 Pet. 5:6).

The honour of the God of Israel having been fully vindicated, Elijah was told by the angel to go with the captain, fearing nothing. Behold then the prophet with his rough hairy mantle going with his considerable militay escort to the royal palace! To his face he told the wicked king that there would be no recovery for him; he would surely die. "Thus saith Jehovah." Unmolested, the prophet walked out!

Note the sequel:– "So he died according to the word of Jehovah which Elijah had spoken" (2 Kings 1:17). "And Elijah went up by a whirlwind into heaven" (2 Kings 2:11). Tremendous contrast!

★   ★   ★

In the world's last crisis, after the removal of the heavenly saints, heavy judgments will reappear at the call of the servants of God. In Rev. 11 we read of witnesses in Jerusalem who will perform the same terrible miracles as Moses and Elijah in the past. Also, the martyrs of that period will pray for judgment upon their persecutors (Rev. 6:10). But that period is not Christianity.

Elijah's Translation

THE Holy Spirit delights to tell us in Heb. xi. that the worthies of old time preferred Heaven to Earth. Heavenly counsels had not yet been revealed, nor could they be until after the death and resurrection of Christ and the descent of the Holy Spirit. Old Testament saints were partakers of an earthly calling; but they were so deeply sensible of the ruin of everything here as the fruit of sin, and of the impossibility of flesh ever repairing the mischief it has wrought, that their hearts rose up to Heaven. God was their hope, and their affections were set where He dwells. They "confessed that they were strangers and pilgrims on the earth"; they desired "a better country, that is, a heavenly: wherefore God is not ashamed to be called their God: for He hath prepared for them a city" (Heb. 11:13-16). In that city we shall meet them all ere long.

The manner of Elijah's departure from this scene of toil and strife is noteworthy. We recall a moment when he sat under a juniper tree disappointed and depressed, and requested for himself that he might die. Yet the God of all grace had purposed for him a departure from this world such as no other has ever had, the blessed Son of God alone expected. "Enoch was translated that he should not see death; and he was not, for God took him" (Heb. 11:5: Gen. 5:24); but nothing spectacular is suggested in the Holy Spirit's brief record. We – God's present saints – are expecting something far more wonderful than either Enoch or Elijah experienced. Not individually, but in a countless throng we shall be caught up. For this the Lord will come in person (1 Thess. 4:16-17). Oh, the unspeakable blessedness of "the coming of our Lord Jesus Christ, and our gathering together unto Him!" (2 Thess. 2:1). What an end for all the anxieties and sufferings of earth!

Elijah's removal was known in advance by many persons. At least fifty-one men were interested in the great event, but only one witnessed it (Elisha); and he only, so far as we can gather, got a blessing out of it. The sons of the prophets were very sceptical about the miracle; and, although they were discouraged by Elisha, they sought diligently to find Elijah's body. Why are men so dubious of divine miracles? Why should they doubt the power of God? Alas, the fifty young men who searched for Elijah's body were all "candidates for the ministry!" What a foreshadow of what has become very common in our day!

Elijah's translation must be regarded as a mark of Jehovah's approval of His servant who witnessed for Him so bravely in a very evil time. His dealings with Elijah at Horeb, when for a moment his faith broke down, were private. The record of what passed there was afterwards written for the instruction of others who might come after.

The prophet's last journey requires careful examination. It commenced from Gilgal, Elisha accompanying him. Jehovah could easily have taken up His servant from Gilgal itself; instead, He led him about; first to Bethel; next to Jericho, and then across Jordan. It was a kind of retracement of Israel's steps in the days of Joshua. God would in this way present vividly to Elijah's mind the hopeless evil of the people he had served so well, and who had caused him so much grief and disappointment. Gilgal was Israel's first camping ground after they crossed the Jordan. There they signified their dependence upon God by circumcising themselves in the very presence of the foe

(Josh. 5). The place was now one of Israel's chief centres of idolatry. "All their wickedness is in Gilgal" (Hos. 9:15). "At Gilgal multiply transgressions" (Amos 4:4). BETHEL had sacred associations as the place where Jehovah made himself known to Jacob in His faithful love. He said: "this is the house of God, and this is the gate of heaven" (Gen. 28:17). Now one of Jeroboam's calves stood there, in public defiance of Jacob's God! JERICHO witnessed the power of God at the beginning; its rebuilding was glaring evidence of the people's infidelity (1 Kings 16:34). Thence Elijah crossed the Jordan; and from outside the limits of the land he was rapt by divine power to heaven.

His years of testimony, with striking miracles accompanying, were a warning to the nation; the conduct of Ahaziah and his officers was a solemn proof that the warning was unheeded. But God delights in long-suffering. He is never hasty in judgment. He even granted respite to wicked Ahab when He saw him lying low in sackcloth after the murder of Naboth; and even now although He was withdrawing Elijah from the scene of testimony, He gave His wilful people another opportunity in the gracious ministry of Elisha. But it was all of no avail; and in due course the blow fell. The kingdom was destroyed; and the people were swept out of their land into captivity. The terrible "Lo-Ammi" sentence has not yet been recalled; nor will it be until the appearing of the Lord Jesus.

There was not only a voice to Elijah in the steps of his last journey; there was also a voice to Elisha, who was to witness for God in the land after Elijah's departure. Elisha had an impression that there was a meaning – a meaning of spiritual value – in the movements of that day. Thus he kept close to the departing one, not permitting himself to be deflected, either by the words of the prophet, or by the remarks of the sons of the prophets. Three times Elijah said, "Tarry here, I pray thee"; but Elisha replied each time with holy fervour: "As Jehovah liveth, and as thy soul liveth, I will not leave thee." It was not that Elijah wished to get rid of his friend; but he would test his constancy. Barnabas counselled the converts in Antioch to cleave to the Lord with purpose of heart (Acts 11:23). Blessed counsel; may we all heed it! Both joy and power depart when we allow anything to come in between our souls and the Lord. Paul walked once from Troas to Assos – about 25 miles – alone, sending his companions round by sea (Acts 20:13). He had his own reasons for avoiding conversations just then. With Elijah and Elisha it was different. "They still went on, and talked" (2 Kings 2:11). Elisha was bent on getting the full blessing of that wonderful day. Like Paul later, he would have said: "This one thing I do, forgetting those things which are behind –" (Phil. 3:13).

GILGAL, as we have seen, was the starting point. There the men of Israel used sharp knives upon themselves after they had crossed the Jordan. This was God's way of teaching them that He can give no recognition to the flesh; it is evil in His sight beyond repair. Have we in spirit crossed the Jordan? Have we definitely accepted the death of Christ as our own, so that we can intelligently hear the apostle saying to us, "If ye then be risen with Christ, seek the things which are above where Christ sitteth on the right hand of God?" (Col. 3:1). As surely as Elisha ws appointed to represent the prophet who had gone up to heaven, so we have been divinely set to represent the glorified Christ. But in order that this may be we must be severe with all the workings of the flesh, hence the words in Col. 3:5, "Mortify your members which are upon the earth."

After the men of Israel had circumcised themselves, Jehovah said: "This day have I rolled away the reproach of Egypt from off you" (Josh. 5:9). Gilgal means "rolling." Everything that is suggestive of the world; everything reminiscent of our ways when we were in and of the world is a reproach to us. Let us never forget this.

BETHEL was the next haltingplace. What a lesson of God's faithfulness could be learnt there! When Jacob was in flight from home because of his lying and deception, Jehovah appeared to him by night, and assured him of His continued interest and care. He spoke of the land; his seed; and his own personal needs (Gen. 28). Thus if we learn at Gilgal that flesh is always evil, we learn at Bethel that God is always good. the late J. B. Stoney once said: "I know enough of flesh to distrust it utterly; I know enough of the blessed God to trust Him fully." It gives strength to any witness for God to be able to speak thus.

From Bethel the two prophets went to JERICHO. When Joshua led the hosts of Israel into the land Jericho was a key city, strongly fortified. They could not by-pass it; but they had no need of military machinery for its destruction. Jehovah manifested His power by causing the walls to fall down flat. Hiel the Bethelite rebuilt it in Ahab's day. In like manner men are frequently seeking to rebuild that which has crashed as the fruit of their sins (Isa. 9:9-10). But all the wit of man could not lift the curse which lay upon Jericho. The situation of the city was pleasant; but the residents were obliged to confess "the water is bad, and the ground barren" (2 Kings 2:19). God is the great restorer; oh, that men could understand it!

After Jericho, Elijah and his friend reached the Jordan, and by the power of God they passed through

the river dry-shod. Jordan being a type of death, Elijah
and Elisha typically passed through death that day on to
resurrection ground. The lessons of all these places
should be grasped by our souls if we are to be efficient
witnesses for the absent Christ. The badness of the flesh
which calls for the knife continually (Gilgal); the
faithfulness of God (Bethel); the power of God over all
the might of the enemy (Jericho); and the great lesson of
death and resurrection with Christ as taught in Col. 2.
and 3.

On the eastern side of Jordan Elijah said to Elisha
"Ask what I shall do for thee before I be taken away
from thee." A test question, assuredly, reminding us of
Jehovah's word to Solomon in 1 Kings 3:5. Elisha's
reply was prompt and decisive: "I pray thee, let a
double portion of thy spirit be upon me?" Elijah spoke
with authority. At this point he typifies the risen Christ
who has boundless blessings to bestow upon His own.
Elisha could have what he desired on one condition; he
must see Elijah when taken from him. Faith now sees
Chirst risen and glorified. Had we known Christ after
the flesh, i.e. as a living Messiah, we know Him as such
no longer (2 Cor. 5:16). He has "gone into heaven, and
is on the right hand of God" (1 Pet. 3:22). We are "in
Him" there. This makes us heavenly as He is heavenly
(1 Cor. 15:48). Elisha did see his master taken up, and
received his mantle as it came down upon him. The
risen Christ has sent down to us the Holy Spirit (John
16:7). We thus have the same power for life and
testimony as the man Christ Jesus had when here
amongst men.

What a sight Elisha beheld! "There appeared a
chariot of fire and horses of fire, and parted them both
asunder: and Elijah went up by a whirlwind into
heaven." The one who was left exclaimed: "My father,

my father, the chariot of Israel, and the horse thereof!" He felt that the people themselves were too blind to understand it. In like manner the saints are today the world's most precious asset, whether men perceive it or not. Having received Elijah's mantle, Elisha rent his own clothes in two pieces. If we, God's present saints, are truly conscious of our union with the risen Christ, we will desire that nothing of ourselves shall again be seen. Our whole deportment should speak to men of Christ.

Elisha recrossed Jordan in order to begin his great work in Israel. Smiting the waters with the mantle, he cried: "Where is Jehovah, the God of Elijah?" and the waters parted before him. The honoured servant had gone but God remained. This is always true. Men fill their little day, and pass from us; their memory is precious; but God ever remains with His people. Elisha enjoyed angelic ministry as well as Elijah; for when the Syrians besieged Dothan with a view to taking him prisoner, the mountain was full of horses and chariots of fire round about him (2 Kings 6:17).

The sons of the prophets said of Elisha when they saw him, "the spirit of Elijah doth rest on Elisha," and they bowed low respectfully before him. May it be ours to be respected, not for our learning or wealth, or social dignity, but for the power of the Spirit of Christ manifested in our lives!

On the Holy Mount

VERY few men have been sent back to earth after having left it. Three are noted in Scripture:– Samuel was sent (not in response to the call of the witch) to pronounce the doom of Saul (1 Sam. 28); and Moses and Elijah were sent to greet the Father's well-beloved Son on the Mount of Transfiguration. A great honour for them, and full of meaning for us.

There was a general feeling in Israel that Elijah would come back. Mal. 4:5 was ample authority for this expectation. Among the questions put to John the Baptist was, "Art thou Elias? And he saith, I am not" (John 1:21). When the Lord Jesus challenged His disciples as to what the people were saying about Him, they replied, "Some say thou art. Elias" (Matt. 16:13-14). When He cried out in anguish upon the cross, the bystanders said "He calleth for Elias . . . let us see whether Elias will come to save Him" (Matt. 27:45-49).

Well – Elias (Elijah) did come to see our blessed Lord, not to Calvary to save Him, but to the holy mount to honour Him. That wonderful outshining of glory was witnessed by three of His disciples for the strengthening of their faith; for they were perplexed by His lowly bearing amongst men, and also by His references to a cross, all so contrary to what they looked for in the promised Messiah. Peter, when referring at a later date to the great scene on the mount, said, "we have the prophetic word made surer" (2 Pet. 1:19 – J.N.D.)

Several days before the Lord took Peter and John and James to the mountain top He sought to prepare His disciples for a life of self-denial and daily cross-bearing. For their encouragement He spoke also of a day of recompense when He will come in glory, and then added, "Verily I say unto you, there be some standing here, which shall not taste of death, till they see the Son of man coming in His kingdom" (Matt. 16:24-28). These words give us the key to the great vision of glory. It is a picture in advance of the Millennial kingdom, presented more particularly in its heavenly aspect. *Matthew and Mark* say "after six days"; *Luke* says "about eight days after." *Six* is man's number; it speaks of his week of labour; it is refreshing to know that after all man's toil and travail there will be an era of rest and glory. *Eight* is the number of resurrection; the risen Christ will bring the blessing in, and make it divinely secure. *Matthew* says "and His face did shine as the sun." How suited to the Kingdom Gospel! For God's King, when He appears, will be "as the light of the morning when the sun riseth, a morning without clouds" (2 Sam. 23:4). To the God-fearing remnant of that day he will "arise as the Sun of righteousness, with healing in His wings" (Mal. 4:2): *Mark and Luke* dwell upon our Lord's clothing. *Mark* tells us that "his raiment became shining, exceeding white as snow; so as no fuller on earth can white them." *Mark and Luke* present our Lord in His lowly character as Man and Servant; hence the emphasis on that which suggests His perfect purity. *John* – the only one of the four Evangelists who witnessed the glory on the holy mount – omits all reference to it; for it was to him given by the Spirit of inspiration to set forth, not our Lord's conferred glory, but the glory of His divine person.

To the astonishment of the three disciples, Moses and Elijah appeared, and entered into the conversation with the Lord. These prophets could enter more than many into the feelings of the rejected Christ; for both suffered severely from those to whose service they devoted their lives. Luke says the theme of conversation was His "decease (exodus) which He was about to accomplish at Jerusalem." Here we have the only basis of blessing. Moses brought down from God the law to a people to whom He was obliged to say at the close of his life: "Ye have been rebellious against Jehovah from the day that I knew you" (Deut. 9:24). Elijah appeared amongst the people at a critical time and sought to lead them back into the path of obedience. Both Moses and Elijah failed, for flesh is an evil thing. But the One who was about to give His life for sinners could not fail. A Saviour who has passed through death and risen again is the only hope of ruined men. Blessed be His holy name!

Peter was so delighted to see Moses and Elijah in the company of his Lord that he proposed to make three tabernacles, "one for Thee, and one for Moses, and one for Elias"; for he would fain prolong this wonderful meeting. Peter meant well; but in his thoughtless outburst he really dishonoured the Lord. He was almost putting Him on a level with Moses and Elijah! Yet not long before, in contrast with the gossiping multitude who thought that Jesus might be Elijah or one of the old prophets risen again, Peter said fervently, "Thou art the Christ, the Son of the living God" (Matt. 16:13-16). It was true that the three disciples fell asleep when they reached the mountain-top; waking up, they saw the Lord in His glory – the glory of the promised kingdom. As Peter spoke, the bright Shekinah cloud enveloped them all, and the voice of the Father was heard saying, "This is My beloved Son, in whom I am well pleased; hear ye Him." It was right to hearken to Moses and Elijah in their day, for they spake from God; but One whho was infinitely greater than all the prophets had now come. All others must stand aside, and HE must be heard. Remarkably, when Peter wrote his second epistle, and described the vision on the holy mount, he made no mention of Moses and Elijah being present! He had learned his lesson. God was not exalting mere prophets that day; it was upon His beloved Son, despised and rejected by men, He would put "honour and glory." "We were eye-witnesses of His majesty," says Peter enthusiastically, "and the voice which came from heaven we heard, when we were *with Him* in the holy mount."

The outstanding elements of the glory of the coming kingdom were present that day. Jesus was seen in His majesty; with Him were two men, Moses representing the saints who have fallen asleep and who will be raised at the Lord's coming; and Elijah representing those who will be caught up without passing through death at all. A brilliant host of glorified saints will shine forth with the Lord Jesus when He shows Himself once more to the world. The heavenly saints are seen in Moses and Elijah; and the earthly in Peter, James and John. In mortal bodies they beheld the glory of God. The believing remnant of Israel, when they gaze upward at the opened heavens, will say, "Lo, this is our God; we have waited for Him, and He will save us; this is Jehovah; we have waited for Him, we will be glad and rejoice in His salvation" (Isa. 25:9).

While glory was being displayed on the holy mount, a painful scene was being enacted below. A poor child writhing in agony, possessed with a demon, and the poor father bowed down with grief. The coming down of the Lord Jesus changed everything. Satan's power was overthrown, and tears gave place to thanksgiving and joy. Even so will it be in the great day for which we wait, and for which the whole creation groans (Luke 9:37-42; Rom. 8:17-22).

★   ★   ★

"Farewell, Elijah! In our meditations we have followed thee through storm and calm up to the rest and peace of the home of God. It was a great day when thou wast carried upwards in the whirlwind; it was a great day when thou wast sent back to earth for a moment to greet the Son of God; it will be a still greater day when in a mighty throng we shall all surround the throne of God and the Lamb, and fall prostrate before the Lamb, and pour forth the new song that will never grow old: "Thou art worthy . . . for Thou wast slain, and hast redeemed us to God by Thy blood out of every kindred, and tribe, and people, and nation" (Rev. 5:9). No more moments of depression and discouragement; no more peevish longings to die; no more self-occupation; all hearts concentrated upon Him who was the centre of the glory on the holy hill, and who will be the centre of still higher glory for ever. AMEN!"